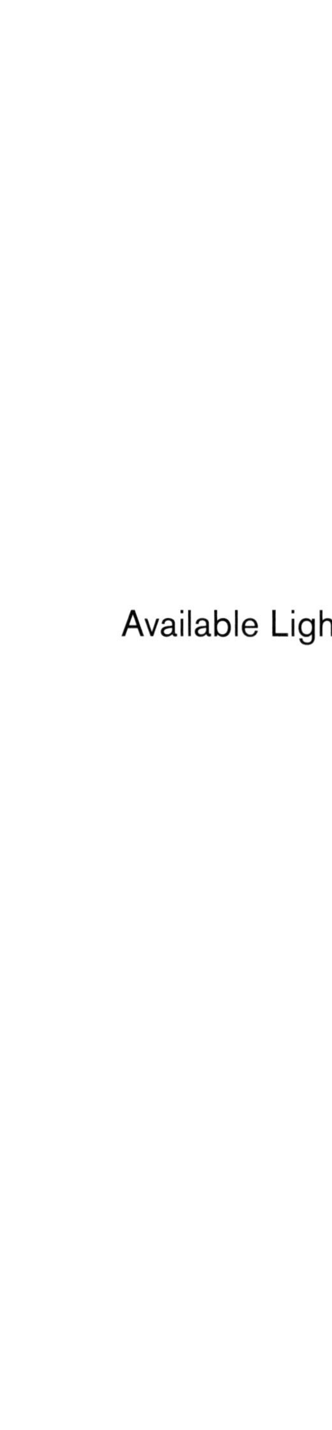

Available Light

Zoe Leonard

Available Light

Dancing Foxes Press / *Ridinghouse*

Contents

The Third Photography

Diedrich Diederichsen

I

A practice, a craft, a medium, an apparatus, a skill, an action—photography can be discussed from all of these angles and from a host of others as well. And like every new invention, it was for the first fifty to one hundred years of its existence. Then the debate became increasingly focused on photography's function in two already existing, extremely varied and institutionalized forms of visual knowledge: art and journalism. This occurred for different reasons, but above all because it became more and more successfully integrated into institutions—museums, galleries, professions, curricula, services, court hearings, etc. The discourse surrounding photography and journalism, with its specific notions of truth, knowledge, and cognition, has recently dwindled to questions of testimony, evidential value, and the authenticity of photographic documents—on the one hand, in the context of an increasing skepticism vis-à-vis subjectivity and, on the other, in the context of digitality. The discourse surrounding photography and art has tended either to reduce photography to just one of many practices available within the art system or else to attempt to salvage it as a "medium" in relation to modernist ideals of medium specificity, as well as to post-McLuhan ideas espousing the primacy of medium over content.

It once occurred to me, while thinking about Zoe Leonard's work, that this state of affairs need not be the final word. Could we not distance ourselves from the reduction that has gradually befallen photographic reflection, since its enlistment in the service of either art or journalism, by accepting its building blocks as historic theoretical concepts but relating them differently? The result would not be something new and untried but something that Leonard has been practicing for some time. On the occasion of these ruminations, I called this phenomenon a "third photography."

Of course, the expression "third photography" took its cue from other "thirds": the Third World, the third sex, the law of the excluded third, the *tertium comparationis*, the Third Wave, and the Third Text. I meant the third photography as not a slogan but a declaration of principles. My idea was primarily that photography's functions in the fields of science and journalism—its role in scientific examination and its role as testimony and evidence—are isolated as principles, as components of modern knowledge and record, and then examined as such in artistic practice: for example, in her work, Leonard brings together similar things as a scientific strategy and, in a journalistic way, preserves contingent traces of everyday life, human and nonhuman, while not exclusively privileging either approach.

Although I continue to think along the same broad lines, my proposition has shifted. Rather than suggesting, as I once would have, that art occupies the third position, localized between a scientific approach and a journalistic one, I would now propose a different triangle of relations that includes art at one vertex and truth and evidence-based practices at another, with Leonard's work occupying the third position.

Analogue (1998–2009) contains a seemingly endless series of, a vast quantity of, storefronts. Both expressions—"series of" and "quantity of"—already imply decisions about the status of the individual photographs and what they depict. (Can one count them? Is it relevant that they are many? Do they constitute a series? Are they a type, a people, a tribe?). One might argue that these storefronts are concrete instances of an abstraction, a concept of the storefront, in the same way that the Bechers' water towers are instances of an abstraction, a concept of the water tower. But this is *not* the case. The differences between water towers are differences between constructional variants that are minimally affected by accidents and contingencies. What is critical is that the deviations are a constitutive element of the elasticity of the concept "water tower" and the construction task associated with it. The merit of the Bechers' project is precisely this articulation.

The differences between the storefronts are of a very different kind. First, as an abstraction, the storefront has no variants. What constitutes the storefront is always the same: a flat, lockable facade that also serves as a surface for lettering. The relevant differences are all found at an additive level—that is, in the lateral proliferation and growth that are not dependent on the storefront's construction but are associated with a quasi-natural development that merely utilizes the template and fills it with something that follows its own logic, a logic that has nothing to do with the construction of the storefront.

That brings us closer to the heart of the matter. There are other photographic series by Leonard (series are by no means the determining factor for my argument but merely an entry point) that are determined by archives, museums, and collections: odd wax models of female anatomy in a Vienna museum; water surfaces seen from an airplane window; graffiti; and used shoes. Perhaps the most famous example is a series of black-and-white photographs of female genitalia that she installed among the paintings in the Neue Galerie at Documenta 9 in Kassel. None of these series present instances of a general concept; rather, they deal with the impossibility of depicting the *real* reality that photography repeatedly confronts within the multiple instances of rendering a concept—hence they show the individual as an instance of something general. At the same time, however, they speak to the possibility of abstraction—that is, the impossibility of forgetting or avoiding the ribbons and twine that unify a concept. For when the nonidentical is the object or even merely the occasion, it depends on techniques of identification.

What can be seen in the extensive series of very different and yet similar photographs of very different and yet similar things—and what does it even mean to speak of "things" in this context? It is associations of a different kind, which can best be described as following the logic of the unconscious. The unconscious rather than nature lets the man-made grow in such a manner that it looks "natural" or contingent but is still clearly recognizable as soul driven and desire dependent. The drives, however, are neither contingent nor natural; they are historical and cultural, but they are historical and cultural in the mode of the not directly accessible. For unlike signs, they have hardware, or "wetware."

Thus, there is something that proliferates and grows, links, combines, and attaches so exuberantly atop the objects that constitute a series in Leonard's work that the typical recedes into the background. Instead, one gets the impression that the nonconstructive logic that causes two (or more) elements to proliferate on a storefront is related to the logic by which the artist is guided as she searches for the next storefront or associates it with the preceding one. How one becomes linked with the other in reality and how one becomes linked with the other in this instance of photography stand in a relationship that may be closer but is in any case more engaging than the mere logic of representation, which of course is also in play.

II

I use the term *subjectivity* here in an unconventional sense: subjectivity is a particular construction with which the world can be experienced in a unique and special way. But it is not in itself inscrutable, and it is not unique. We are all equipped with it. Hence it can be detached from any single person and attached somewhere else. By contrast, individuality is the specific combination of subjectivity with a distinct empirical body. It cannot be moved from place to place. It is our fate, but it is ours alone. The fact that we die is individual; the fact that we know it and may be sad about it is not. Individuals can be counted; subjectivities cannot. At bottom, individuality is of interest to no one. It only becomes interesting when its transferable or communicable aspect—what I am calling subjectivity here—is revealed, most commonly through narration. An escalation of this process of detachment that is not without its dangers is the elaboration of types of subjectivity: distinctive features that occur repeatedly and for the sake of whose clarity other distinctive features are ignored. The perception of types is reduction but also knowledge. Developing types without reduction means incorporating the possible emergence of new types into the representation of a single entity. There can be types of anything, including human beings. In my view, a crucial aspect of Leonard's photography is the way it deals with the countability of what it shows. How often does this exist in the world? The answer is: countless times and just once. It isn't countable, but it is identifiable: for we all identify types without inserting them into a finite system, although we are used to associating knowability with countability, or at least with finitude, and the unfathomable with the innumerable. For Leonard's above-mentioned series, the opposite is true.

Countless times and just once. This is assumed in the scientific-journalistic act of fact-finding by way of a photographic apparatus, a camera, that physically and reliably documents a piece of the world as real. A piece of the world, once and once only. Countless times can only be the result of an act of reception, in which this once-and-once-only is read by someone who has seen something similar before. The series confirms him or her in this view, and other artistic measures reinforce the conviction. Of central importance here is the mode of art, which means: I'm willing to invest my time; I'm prepared to experience an object that reflects someone else's interests; I give it my attention and don't expect anything in return. As a recipient, I am generous. But then I do get something, after all—truth.

One might suggest that, in a certain sense, this is true of all artistic photographs— but it isn't for those that dispense with the journalistic-scientific element, those whose subject is on both levels purely unique (or not unique but countable). However, if we quite attentively consider the "oeuvre of Zoe Leonard," we can find indications that she is validating our perception of this tension: quite early on, for example, in the photographs from airplane windows. Is there anything more unique than these shots—and anything less countable? In this case, the idea does not even need to be realized; it could exist as pure Conceptual art, like a statement written on a wall by Lawrence Weiner.

III

It is an old dream that we not only can know our inner world, understand it, and have a blueprint for it but also can have this knowledge presented to us in a sensuously powerful medium. That is why we once took psychedelic drugs. And that is why so-called serious brain research still uses the peculiar metaphor of the "brain region," by which it purports to explain how mental and cerebral activity is three-dimensional, extended, and spatially defined—as if mere spatial extension were all by itself the way to account for and guarantee the relevance, pliability, and fact of thinking.

But there is something better than a model or a metaphor: we can actually enter and explore the space where the uncountable and the typical meet in the sense discussed above, but do so in a manner that opens up another dimension. Since 2011, Leonard has been making spaces into camera obscuras. They have been sited in public and private art institutions in Cologne, London, Venice, New York, and Marfa, and they enable us to enter a photographic apparatus, to physically penetrate into what it is that makes the above-described phenomenon possible—possible, however, in a very peculiar way. The camera obscura laterally reverses, upends, and projects an image of the environment it faces. But this is no *moment*: the image we see materializes slowly. We perceive it gradually, and then it is there. It is like a film without a storage medium, a film without reproducibility, a film that runs only one time. This singularity, however, is inconspicuous, since it does not escape us that some of what we see upside down and backward is the architecture outside, in other words something stable that does not pass by. The mode in which we perceive this architecture is foreign, not because it appears as a mediated image but because to a certain extent it *doesn't*. It is not a picture, nor is it a film. It does not, in fact, stop being reality. The reality captured in the camera obscura remains reality. An analogous image is that of the image framed by an open window, which seen from a distance can look like a picture until one notices that it isn't, thanks to the stabilities and instabilities and the "ratio" between them, the quotient, which is occasioned only by reality.

IV

As an artist, Leonard is consistent in her focus on certain themes and issues; nevertheless, she does radically different things. What is the connection between her historical and political inquiry into the figure of the bearded lady and her photographs from airplane windows? Given the claims I have made thus far, one might reasonably conclude that what they have in common is a certain idea of realism. It might also be suggested that this very faithfulness to a certain photographic realism necessarily expands photographic practice: a photographer in this sense cannot set photographic practice aside even if it is not an image that is being produced. One must expand the photographic practice to include a series of, at first glance, unphotographic practices of research, installation, and work on and with the archive, as well as a critique of the archive. These activities are relatives of photography.

Indeed, photography is inconceivable without them, but the category all of them occupy is realism.

This realism differs from the kind that is sure of what reality is and what real is and looks for ways to capture it. But it is also not the opposite, the radical constructivist position that there is no preexisting reality and that reality should always be seen as a construction by observers, along with their media, purposes, and pursuits. Instead, it is a realism that acknowledges that reality is impressive but fragile. Reality literally exerts a physical pressure that leaves behind impressions and bruises—but what applies the pressure is nonetheless unstable. Reality affects, indeed overwhelms, us precisely because it disappears a moment later, not because it is so powerful. Its weakness is its strength. This is the only reality that deserves to be sought by the practices of photography. Photography deals not only with imprint or impression but also with disappearance in a deep, technical sense: what it pictures has disappeared at the moment of its relative preservation. In photographs, reality is not preserved absolutely but relatively, in proportion to the fact that the photograph's moment has past. Leonard's camera obscuras walk right up to the limit of this medial disposition, because they expose the conditions of this practice—without rehearsing the various degrees of preservation and disappearance; in this way, the experiences afforded by the camera obscuras frame the photographic exploration of reality as its beginning and its limit. And perhaps it is only a reality explored in this way that deserves to enter into the political questioning of other concepts of reality. (In this way, Leonard's camera obscuras also transcend the melancholy to which photography is prone.)

V

Recapitulation: Leonard's objects are concrete, specific, and often overwhelming. The perception of the objects is fragile and fleeting, but it is based on human action and decision, on subjectivity rather than individuality. These are not expressive images but images that speak of the general element in human seeing and participating. When Goya wrote the sentence "I saw this!" ("Yo lo ví!") or "This is how it happened" ("Asi sucedió") under a drawing in his series *Desastres de la Guerra* (*The Disasters of War*), he was introducing a second subjectivity. The drawing depicted a scene, but a scene that could have been invented. The speaker of this sentence is not necessarily the artist but is a witness, who could have provided his or her account to an illustrator and confirmed its accuracy with these words. In a photograph, however, the identity of witness and artist becomes self-contained. Witnessing, arranging, and responding are three separate acts with associated forms of subjectivity, three different forms of participation whose synthesis seems to become an accomplished fact in the photograph. I often have the feeling that Leonard seeks to separate them and then bring them back together to make the highly specific statement that these very different actions and gestures can coalesce and have coalesced without anything being lost. Individuality, instantaneity, and intention come together here into something that, as subjectivity, is intelligible and applicable for everyone, even those who weren't there, who are other people, and who would never think of depicting this or anything else. The "*I* saw this," the "I saw *this*," and the "*This* is how it happened" are independently knowable and only coalesce in the image—not in the click of the shutter release, the series, or biography and sociology.

But against the single-image synthesis stands the multiplicity of single images, not in all of Leonard's projects but in many. They constitute multitudes of images and things in images that retain a quality of their own. They are arranged like an army, as I noticed when I saw the *Analogue* images installed at Dia at the Hispanic Society in New York. That brought to mind a line from a poem by Conrad Ferdinand Meyer: "We dead are the mightier legions." The uncountability I spoke of returns in the, of course, incalculable number of past and future dead to be grieved who are the natural objects of all photographs, as Roland Barthes pointed out in his essay on photography and the death of his mother. Their ranks swell even further when one considers the dead storefronts (of *Analogue*) in addition to the dead people. Since uncountability is so closely bound up with the internal architecture of Leonard's methodology, from time to time it must shape its external appearance as well.

That which we cannot count but know that we cannot count is the mathematical sublime, a category of aesthetic experience in Kant that makes do without experience: it is enough to think it, or put another way, we can *only* think it, because infinity and uncountability cannot be shown or fully grasped. In a certain sense, Leonard proves Kant wrong by showing that one can see something as a vast army of things and images, which nevertheless do not coalesce into an impression of pure vastness but actually stop short of that mark and remain a multitude of single entities. She is only able to do this because she photographs not from an individual perspective but based on a unified conception of the subjectivities synthesized in the camera: the individual gaze, the fleeting impression, and the practical intention of bearing witness.

VI

There is still one thing that stands opposite all those who cannot be counted, the dead but also those yet to come. Recently, Leonard has begun to repeatedly photograph an object that exists only once and that she can see from anywhere in the world—even if it is sometimes obscured. It is an object that, in its role as something singular, has often been one of religious reverence and is sometimes cited as an exemplar for the monotheistic gods in Judaism, Islam, and Christianity. The Stranglers, the Walker Brothers, and the Beatles have all celebrated it in song: the sun.

But the sun is by no means unique. It is once again an uncountable multiplicity; the inconceivably large quantity of suns in the universe is a subject for astronomy, which actually attempts to count them. At the same time, however, the sun is the source of photography. Leonard claims that to photograph the moon is to replicate the traditional setup in studio photography between subject, light source, and photographer: the moon is lit by the sun to become the subject of the photograph. In turning her camera toward the sun, Leonard merges subject and light source, upsetting the conventional arrangement. The viewer thus becomes implicated and activated in an altered triangulation of relations. I was in the midst of a long engagement with the cultural, ideological, and political significance of the photograph of the whole Earth (the so-called Blue Marble) or of the various photographs of Earth (most of them taken by military equipment) and their role in the peculiar reconciliation of cybernetics and romanticism, hippie culture and the capitalist society of control, when suddenly these photographs of the sun literally threw me off track or out of my orbit.

These images do not simply represent a rebellion against the camera, as it were, the simple, wicked, Oedipal reversal of the very first lesson every photographer is taught: never shoot into the sun. Rather, they are its perfect deconstruction: when you shoot into the light you do not destroy the picture, you get an image of the light source. The latter is no spiritual entity, no "Oh, Lumière!," no torch of enlightenment, but a crazy sphere of gas that really exists. We can see it, wherever on Earth we happen to be; it is always the same, but it is nevertheless not singular. It is only by inverting the idea of illumination, of stepping into the light, that one is enlightened regarding the light source: by turning one's gaze. Light is emitted by this heavenly body but is also emitted by other suns. Illumination, and the knowledge of which it is regarded as the cause, can also be caused by others. Nevertheless, it is massive, overwhelming, and impressive—and unlike almost anything else that can be photographed, it isn't completely different a moment later. It has already been around for more than four billion years and will remain here for roughly five or six billion more, before ballooning into a red giant and shrinking to a white dwarf in the following two billion years (to throw out a few numbers before concluding). The sun is individual, possessing a finite life span like a person, but it is also a component of the architecture of subjectivity per se. Thinking subjectively is like gazing toward illuminated objects. But this construction can be pulled apart and then potentially given back to us. Zoe Leonard grapples with what happens during and after this separation, in all its drama, risk, and surprise.

Translated by James Gussen

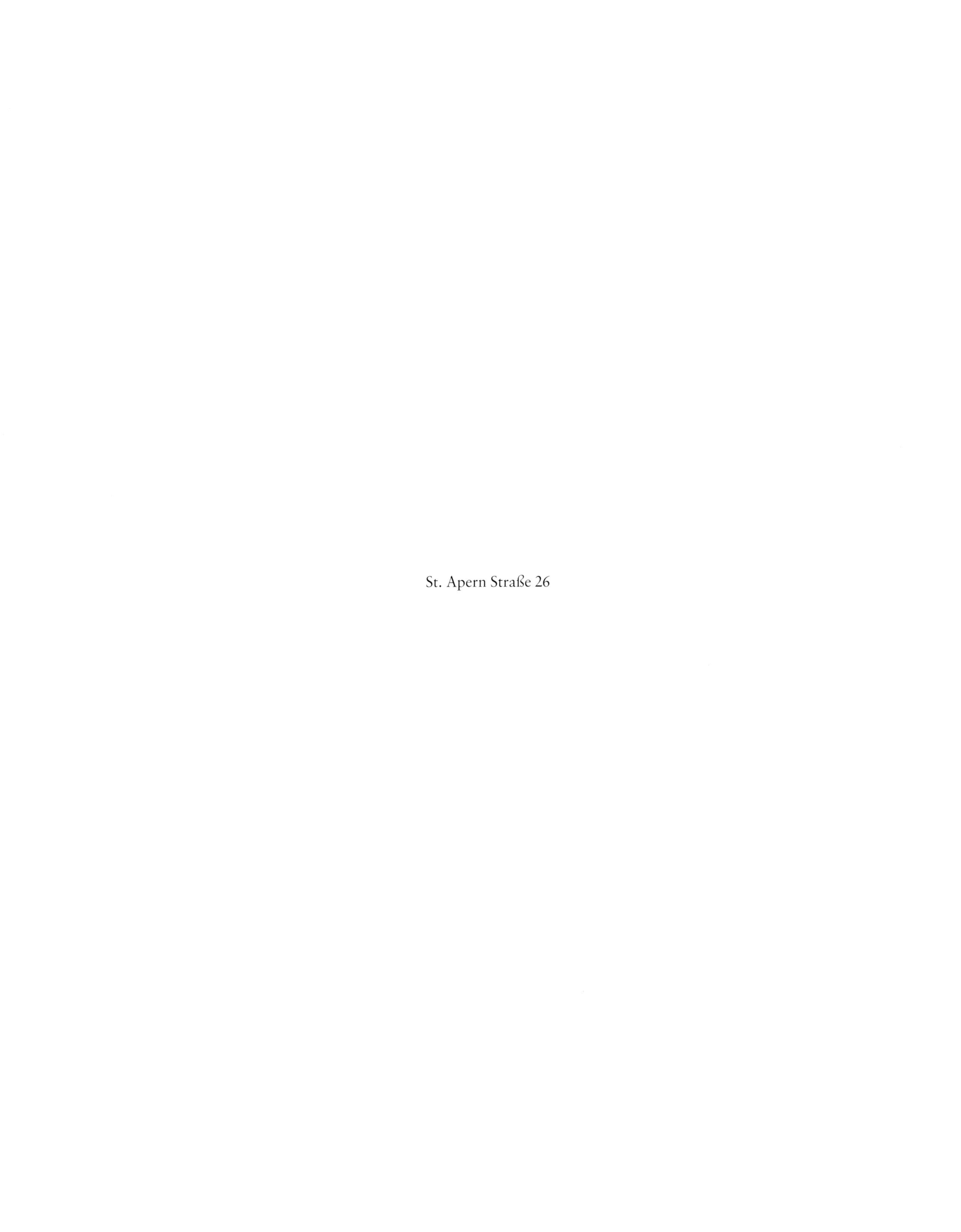

St. Apern Straße 26

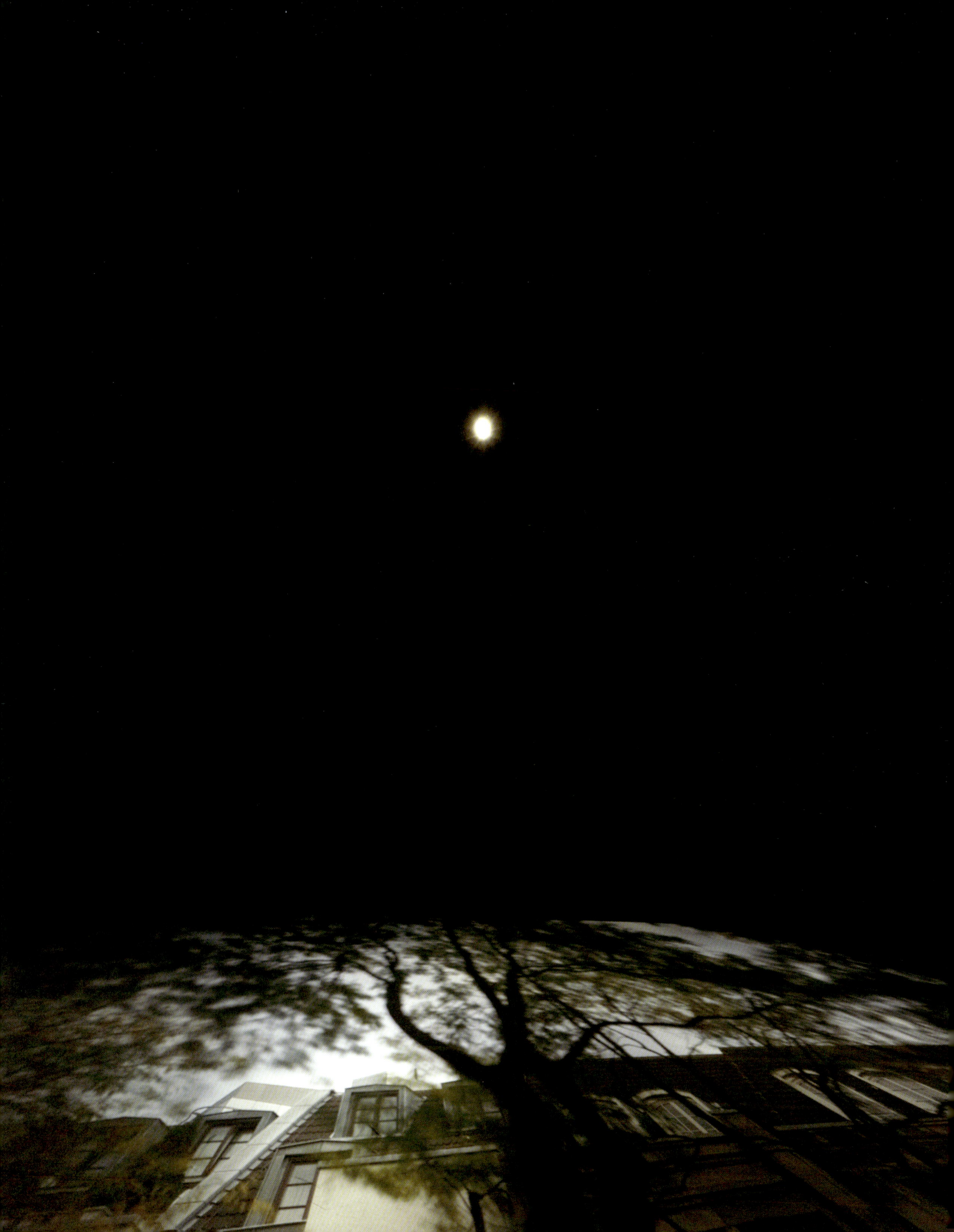

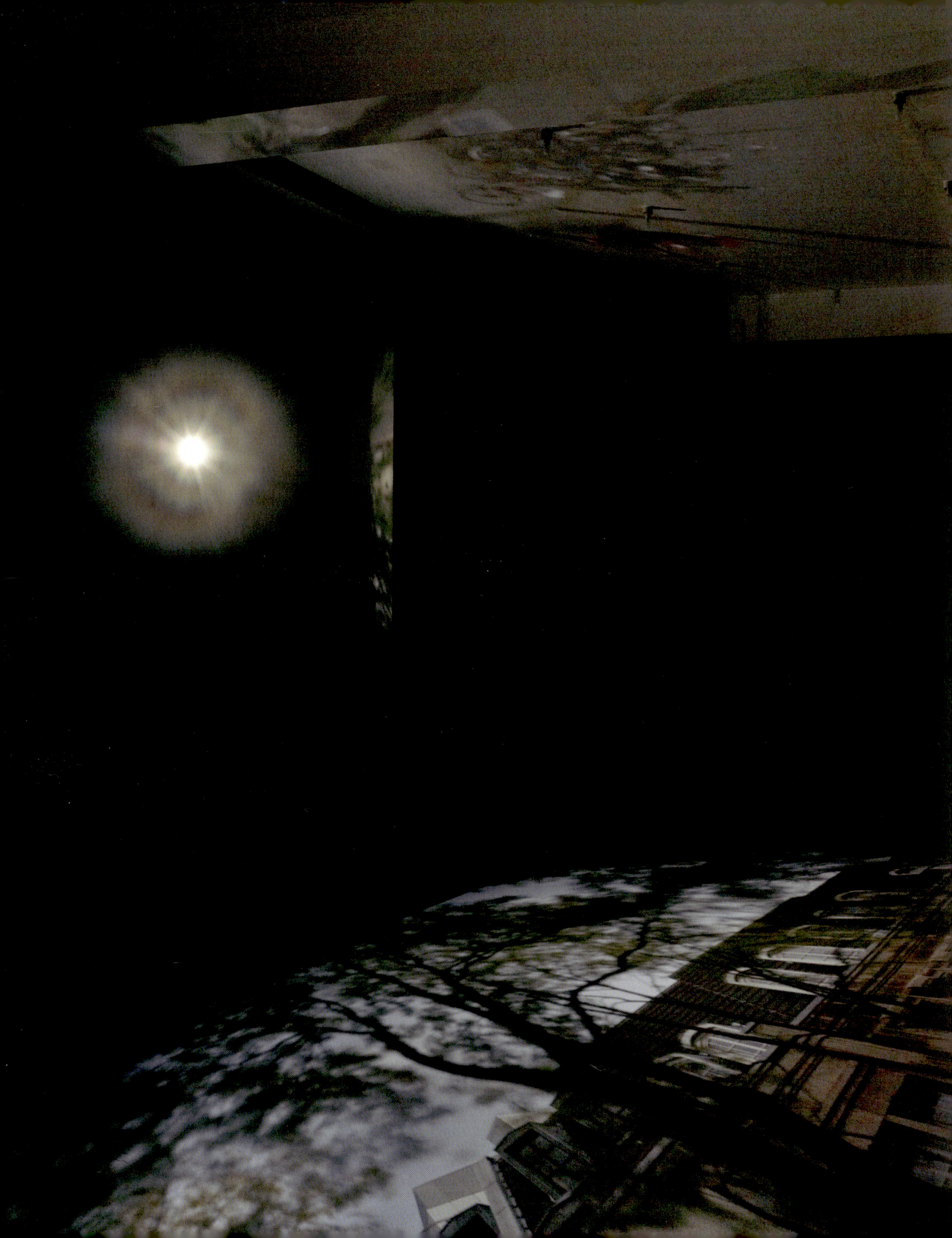

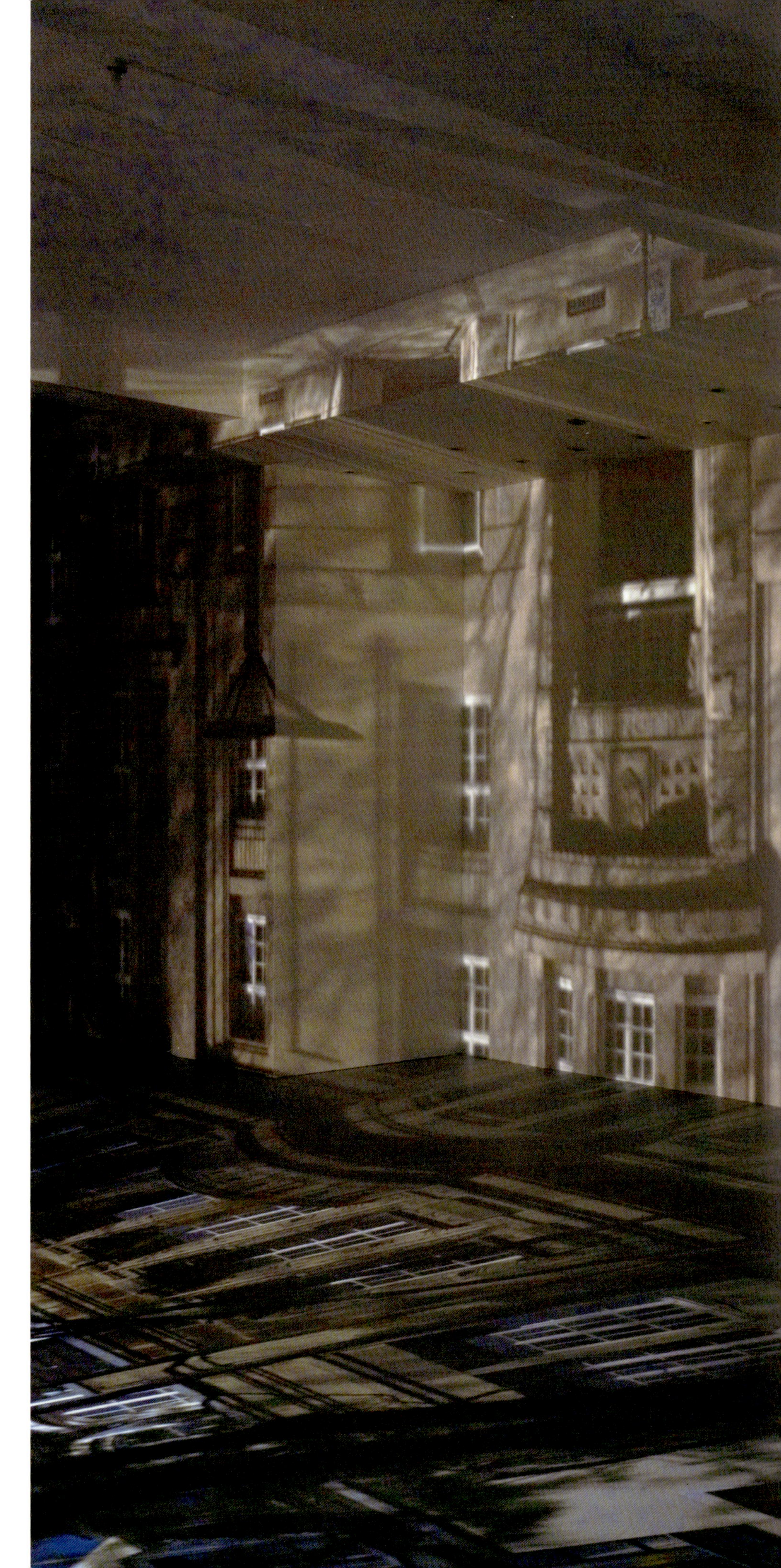

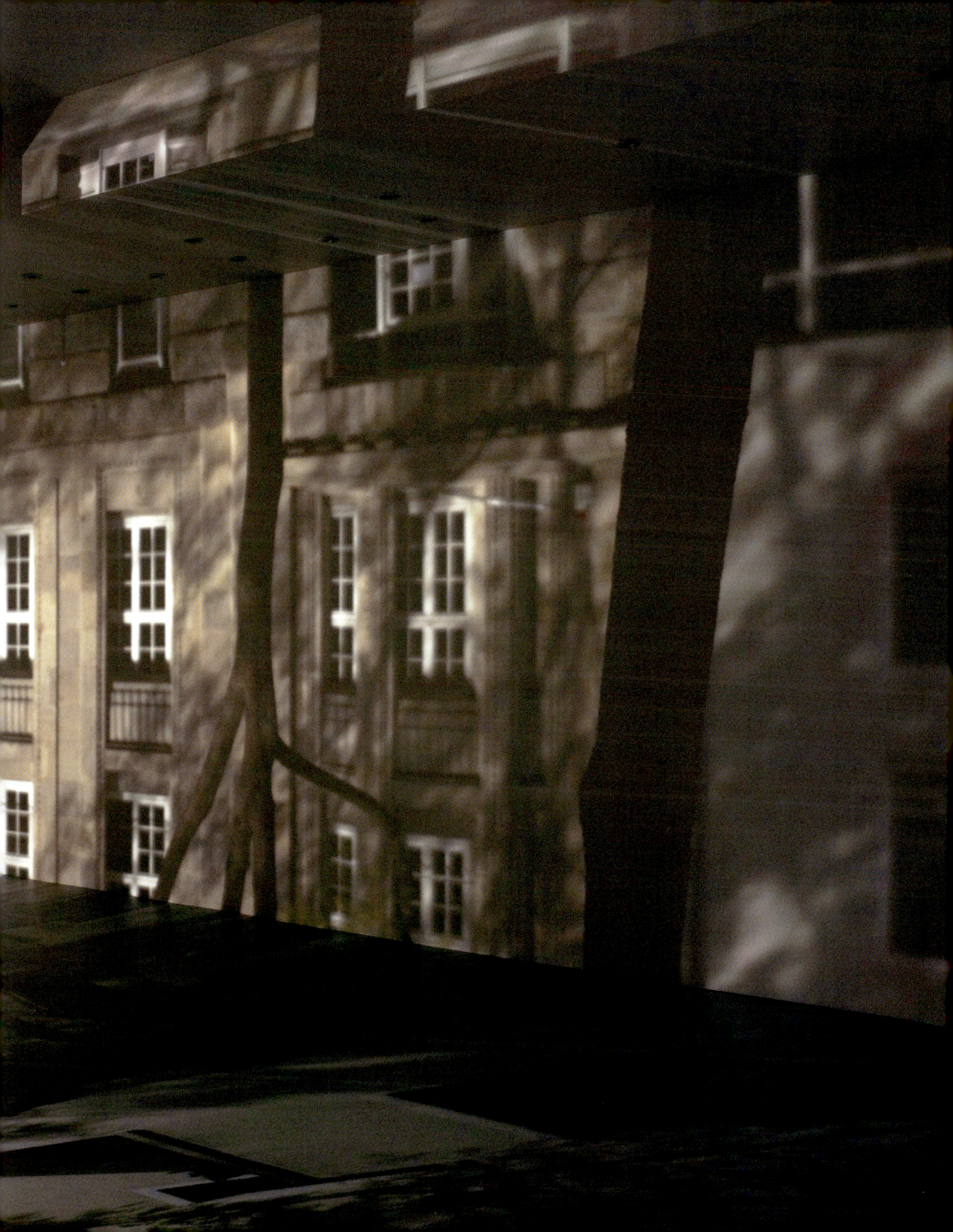

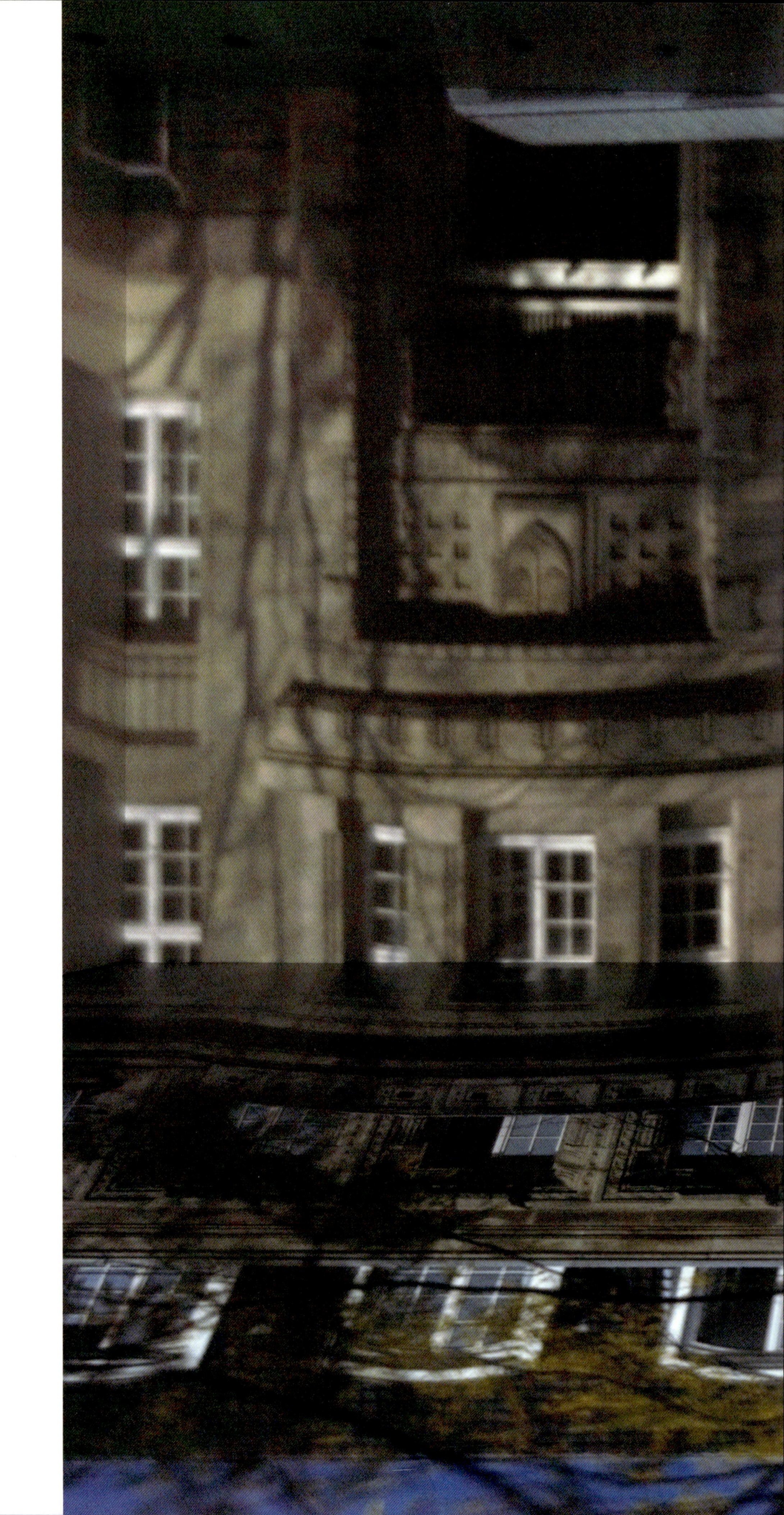

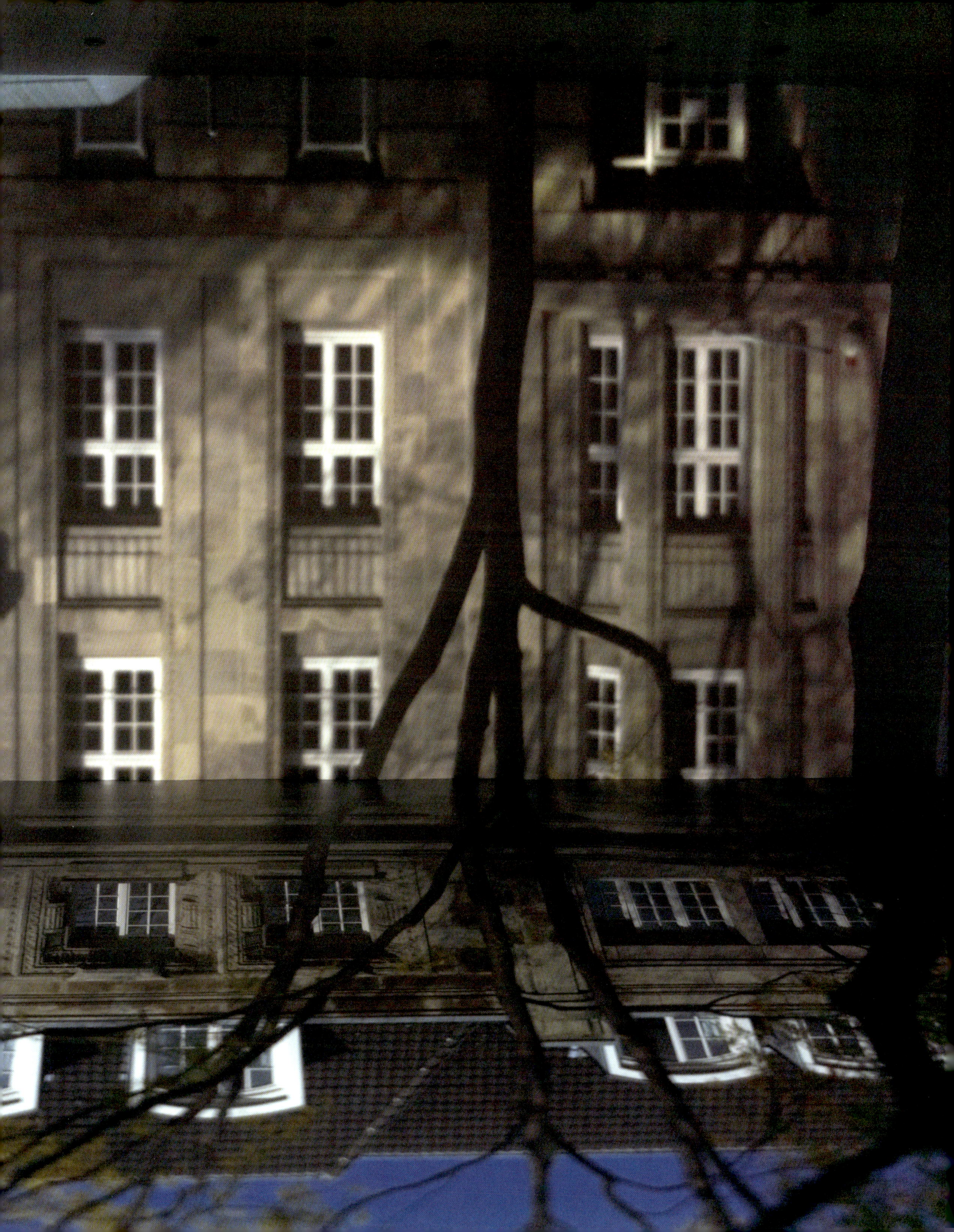

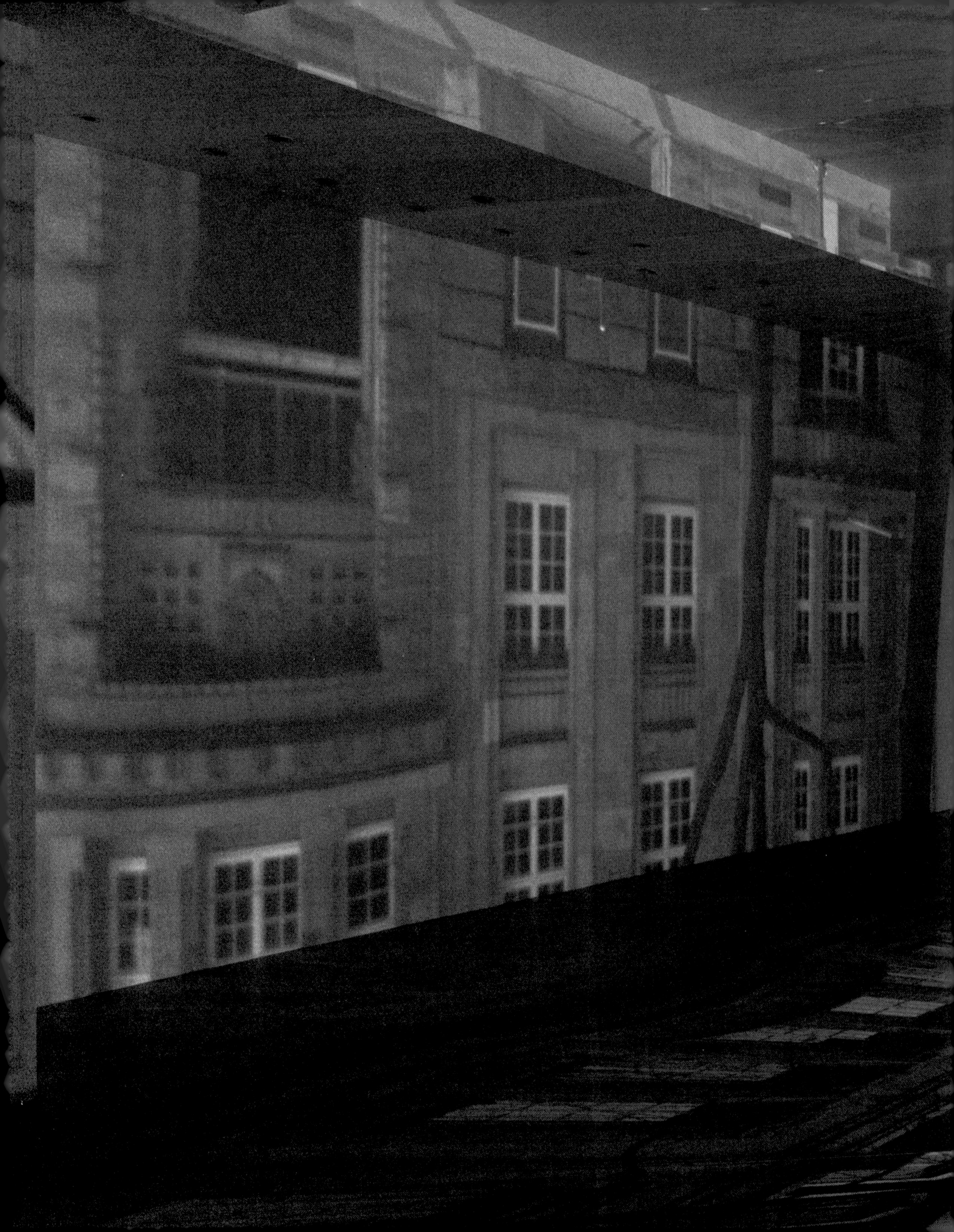

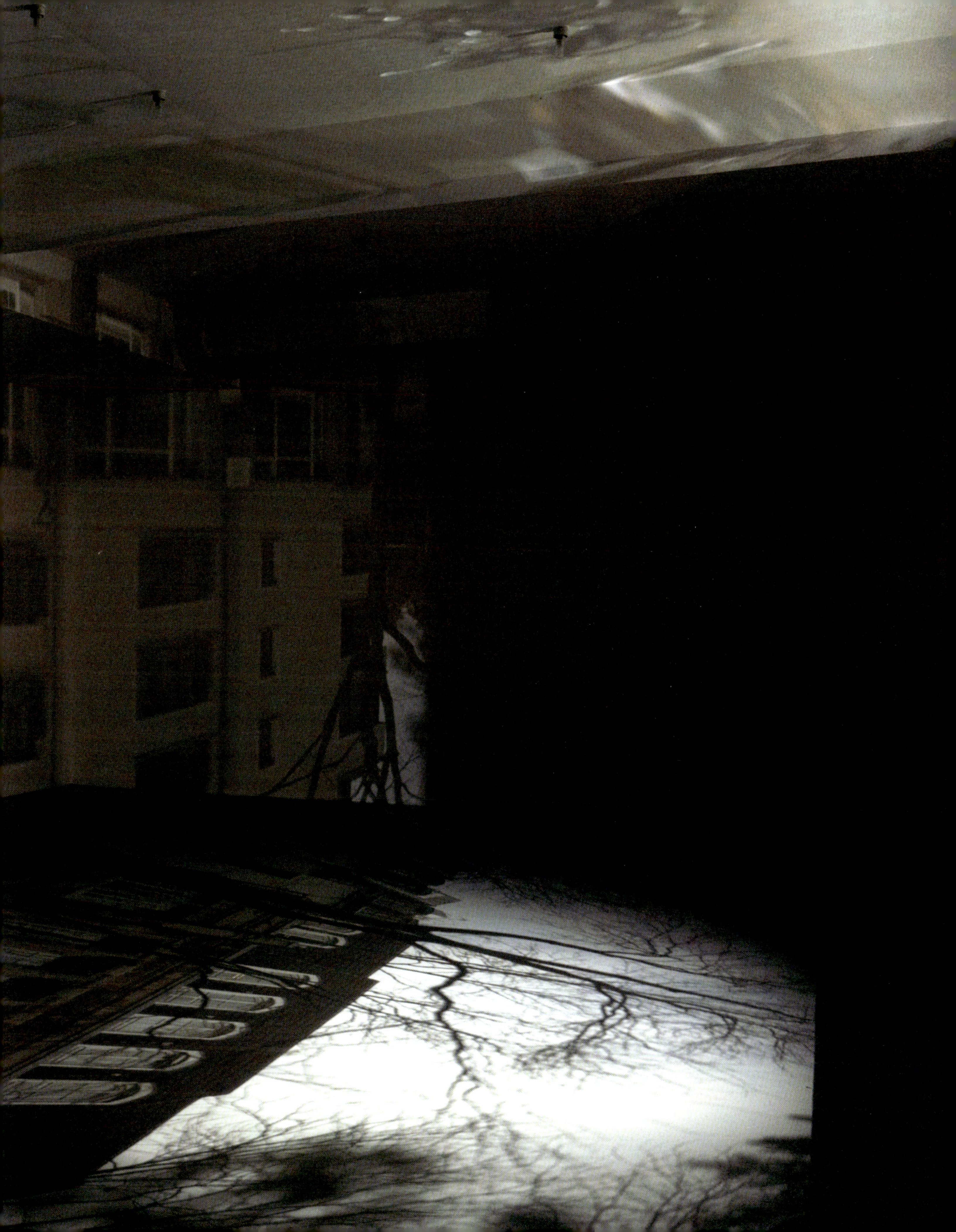

Arkwright Road

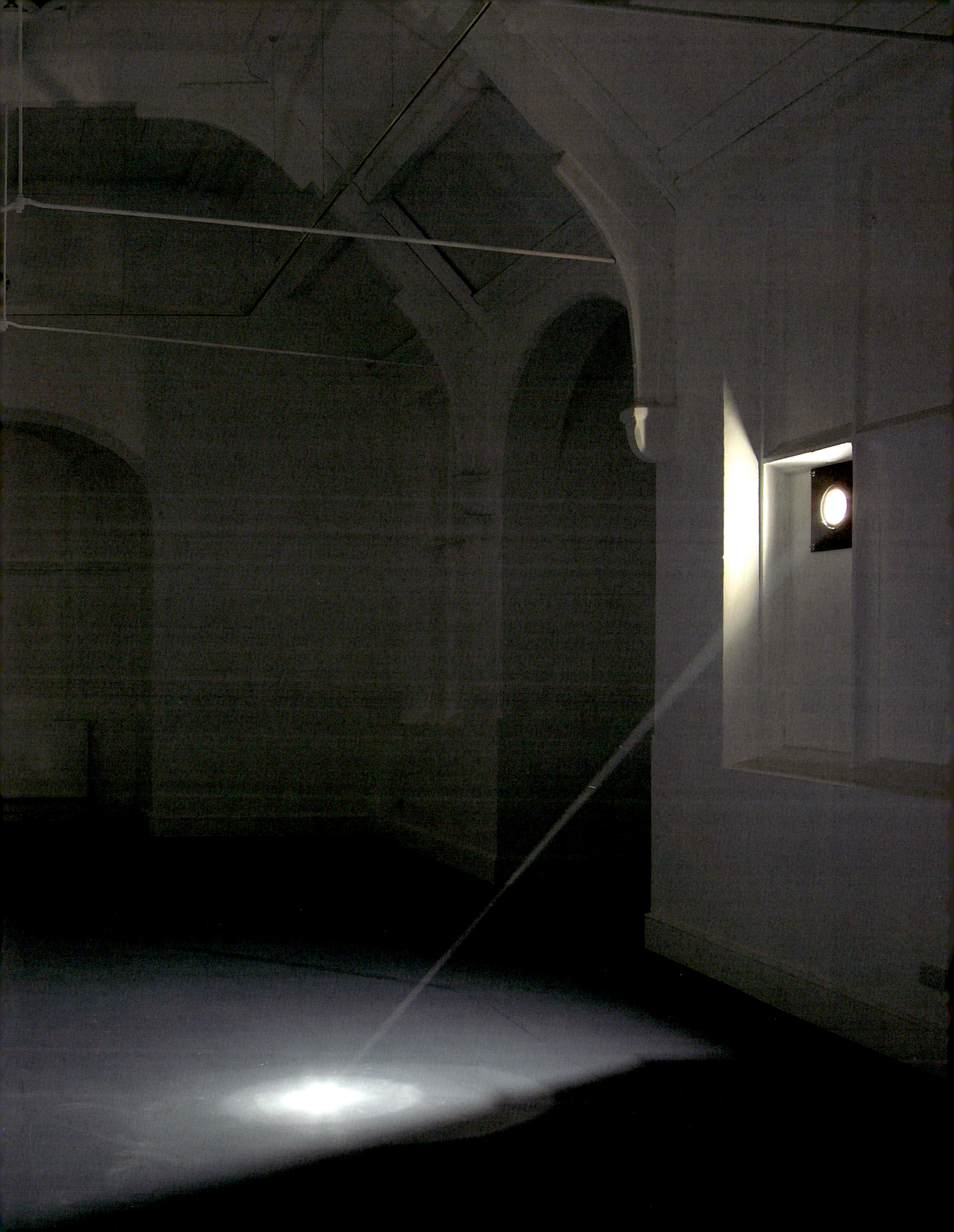

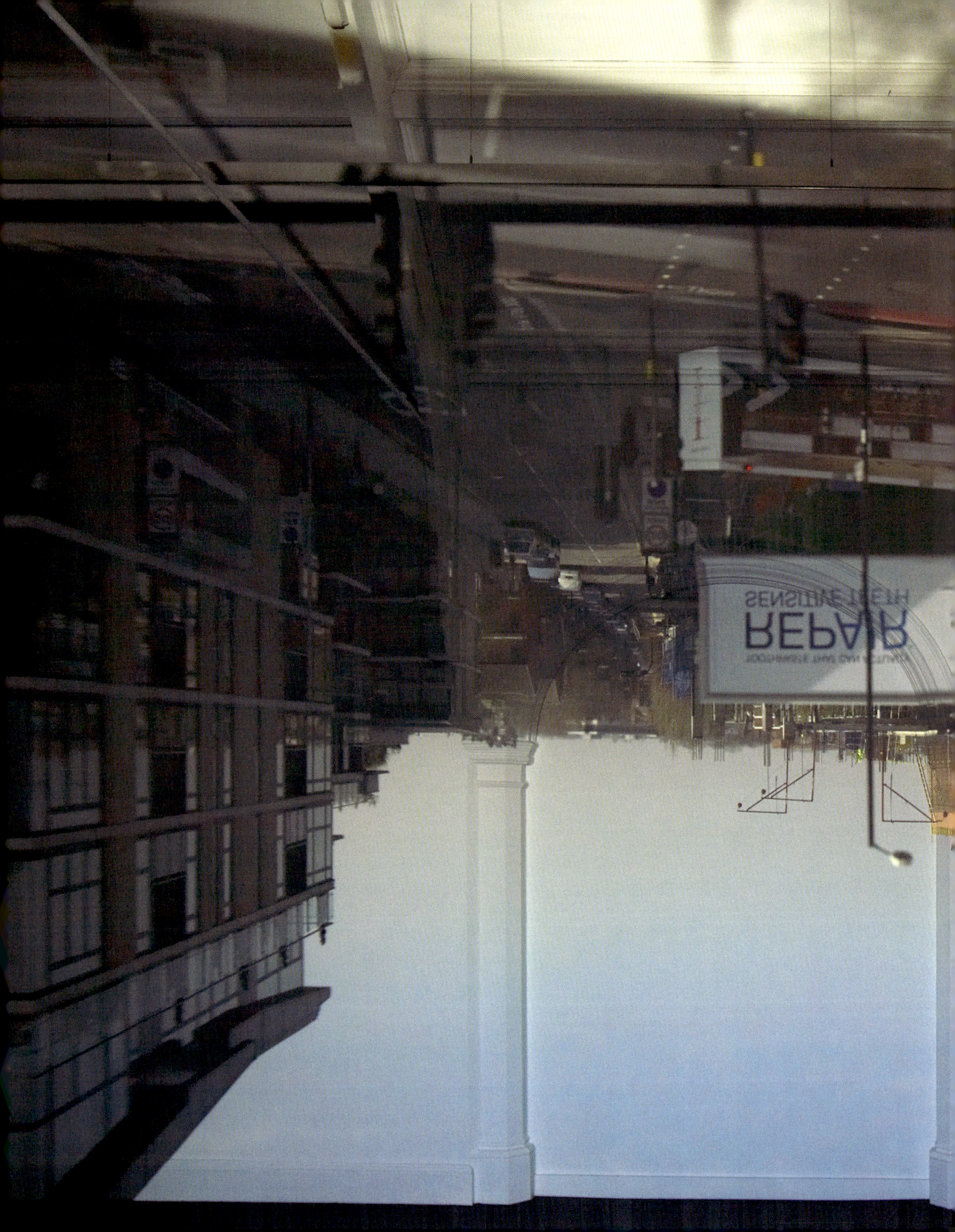

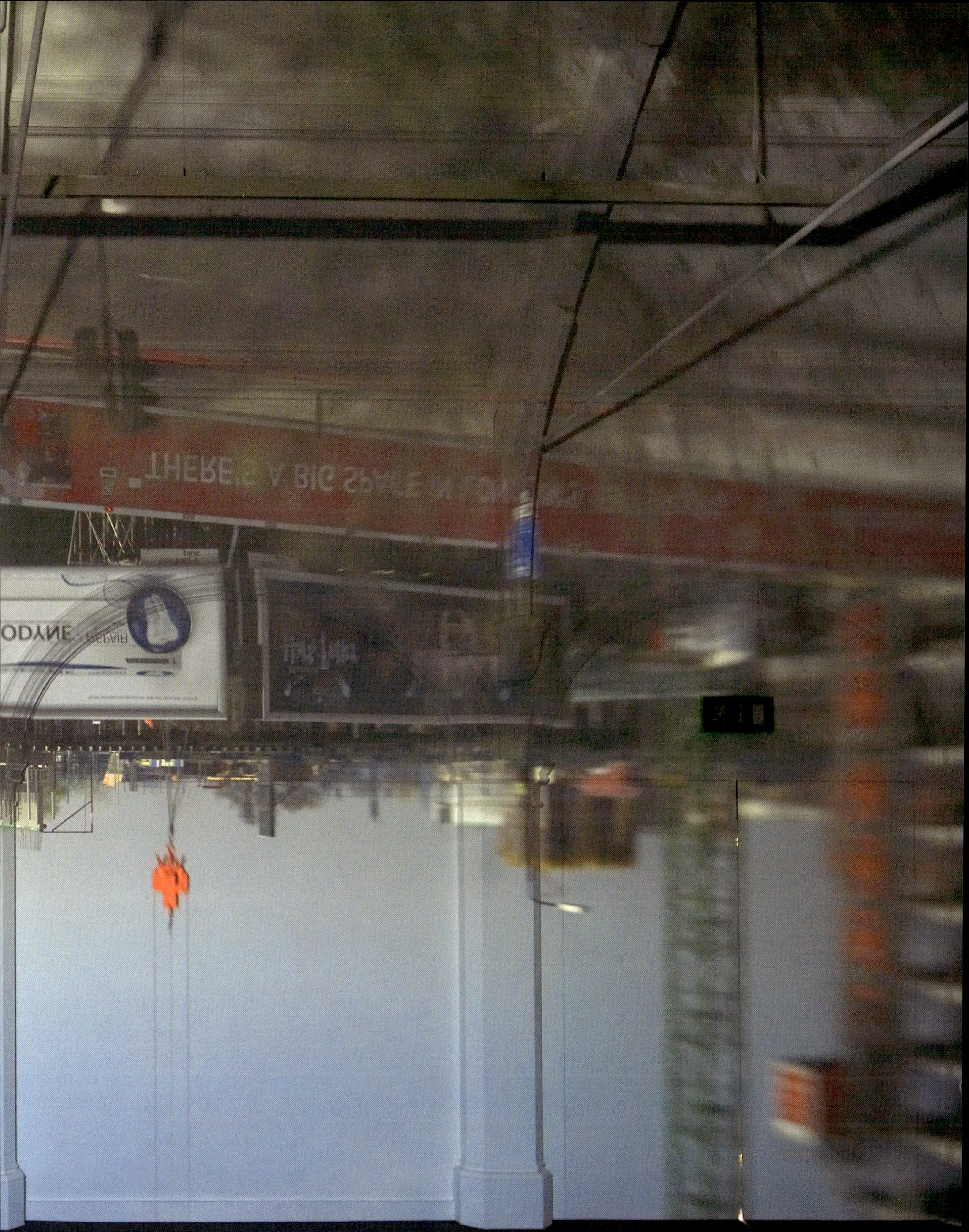

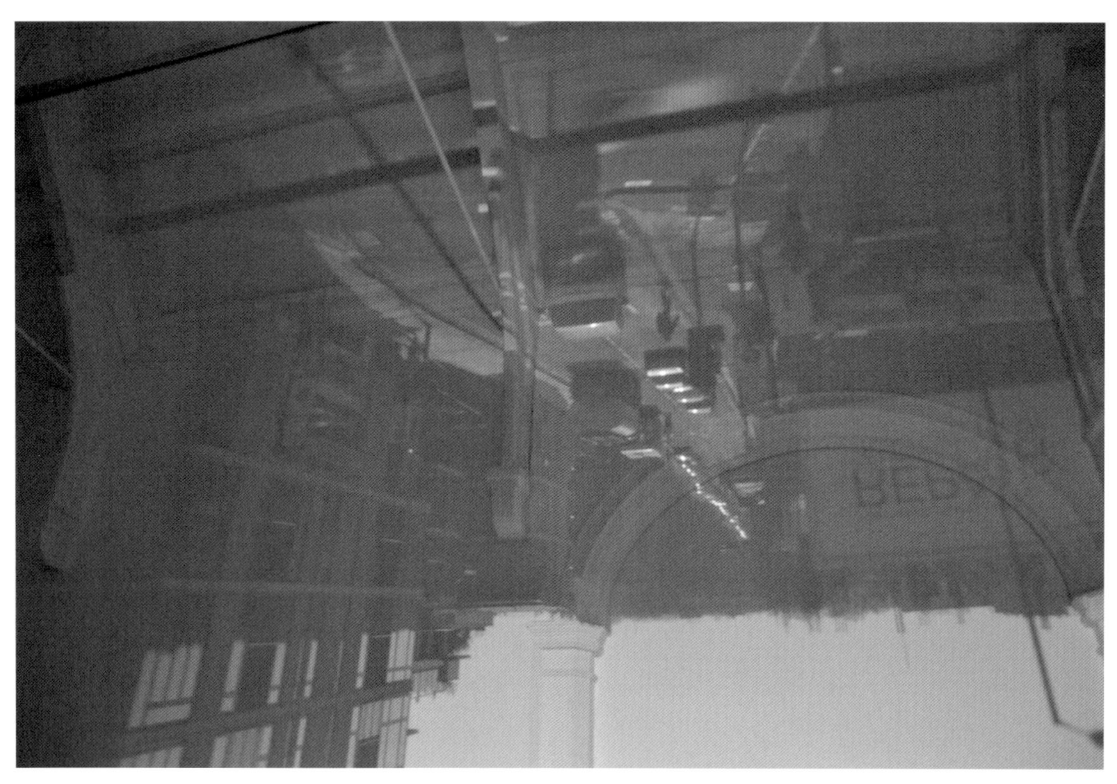

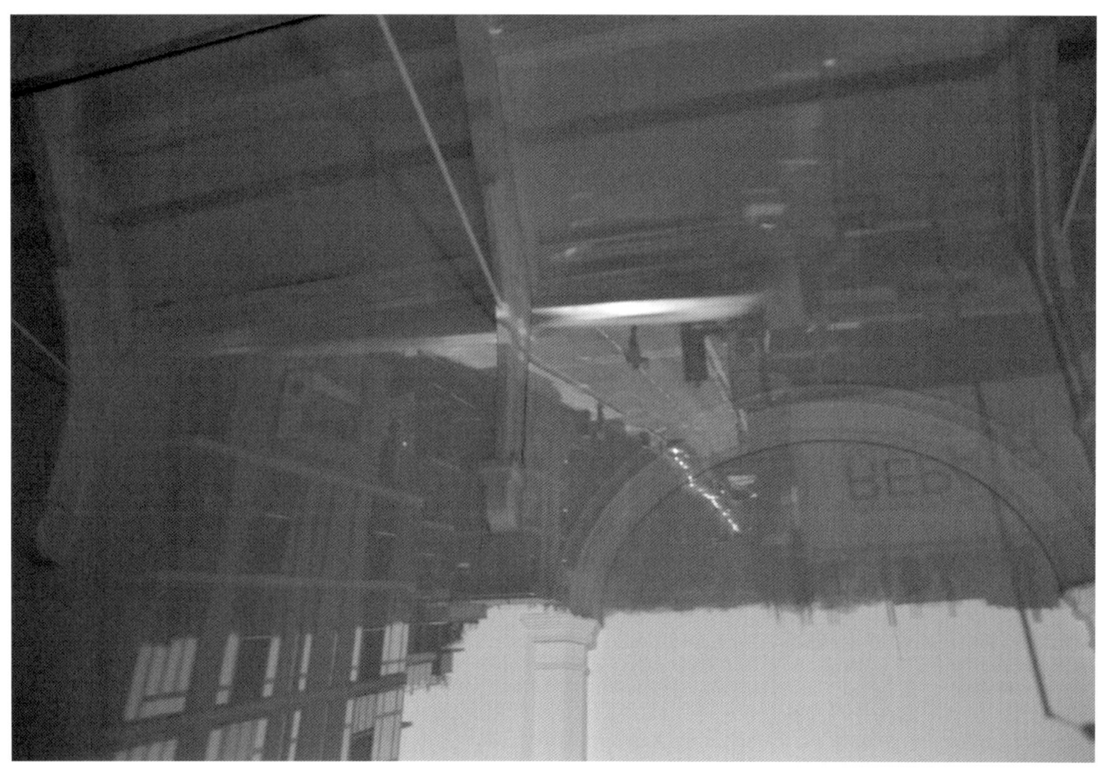

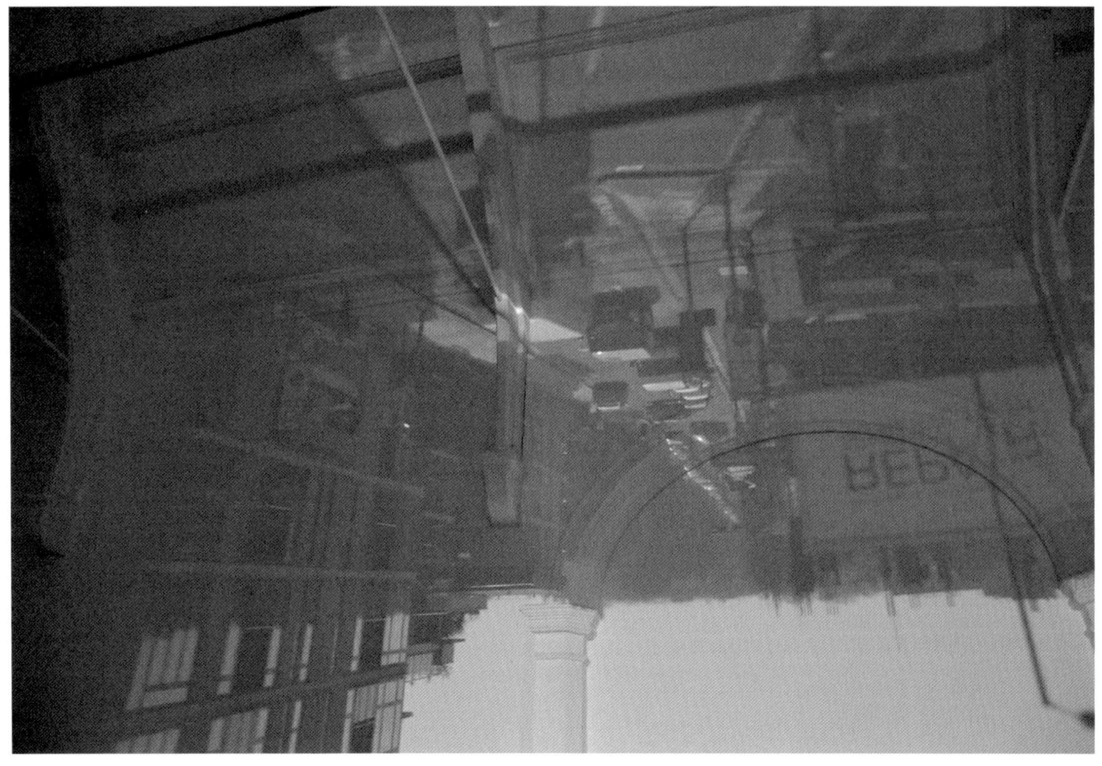

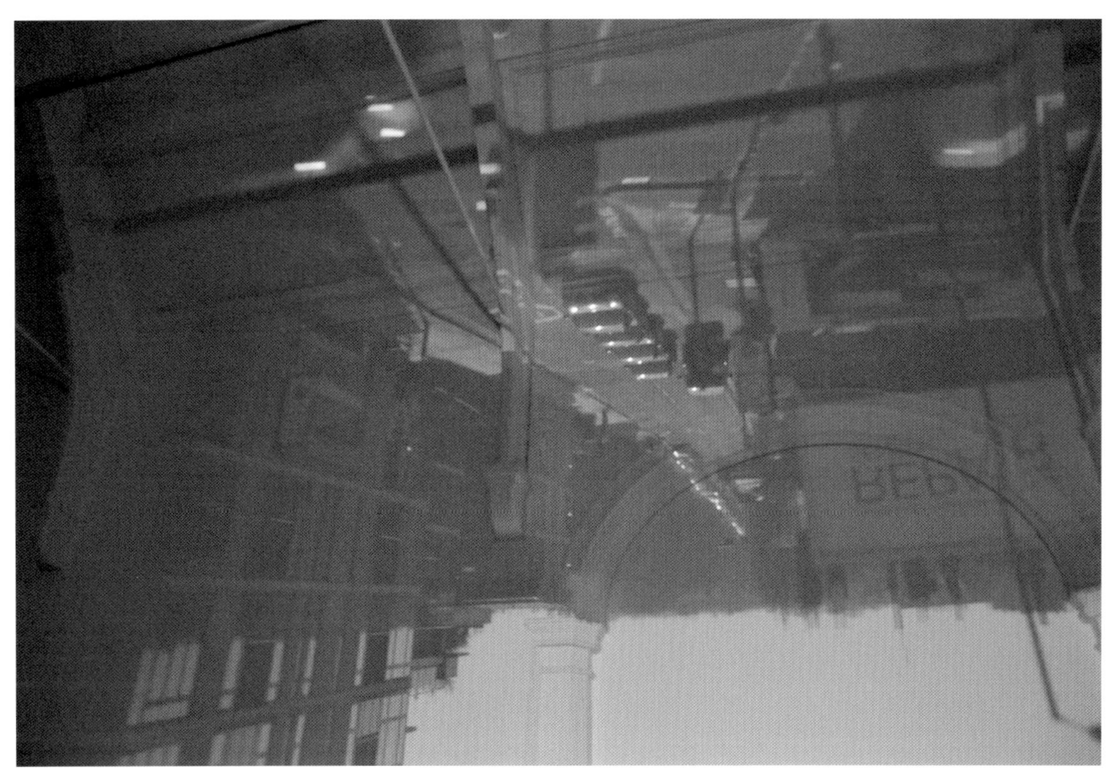

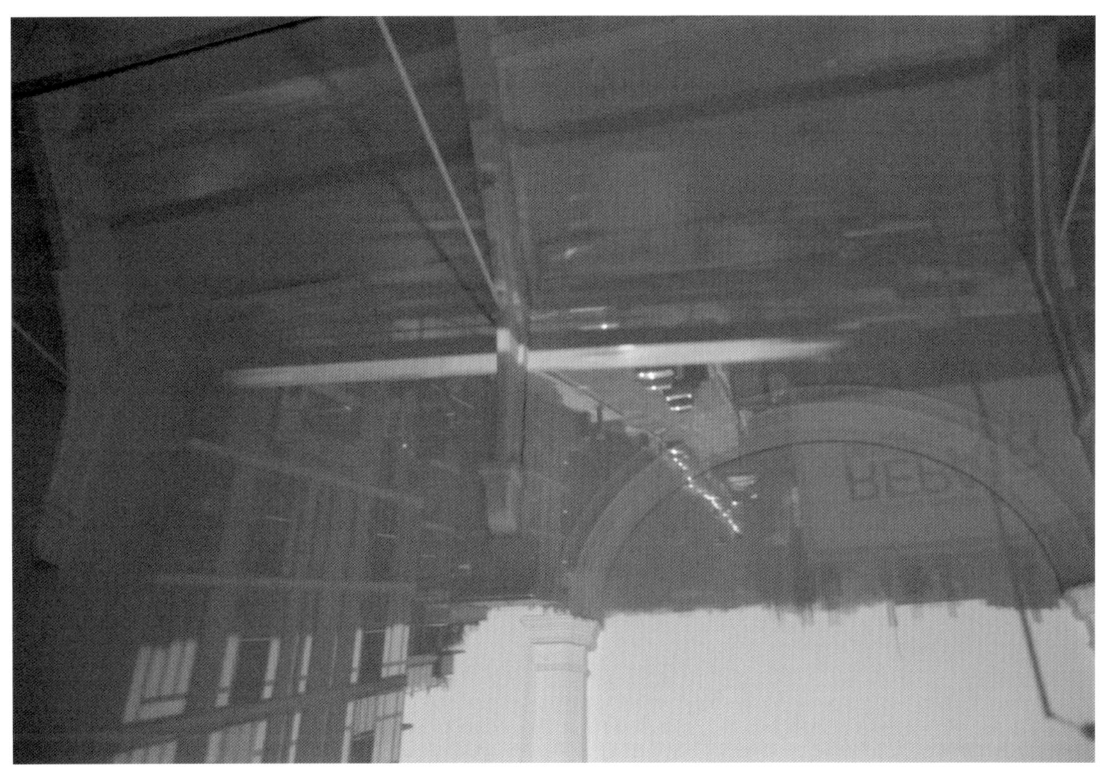

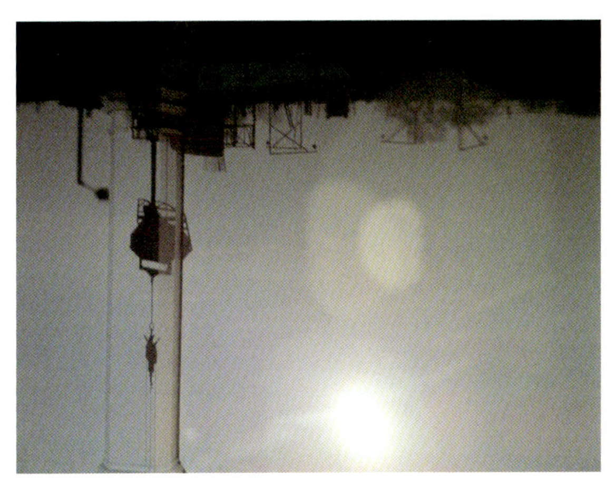
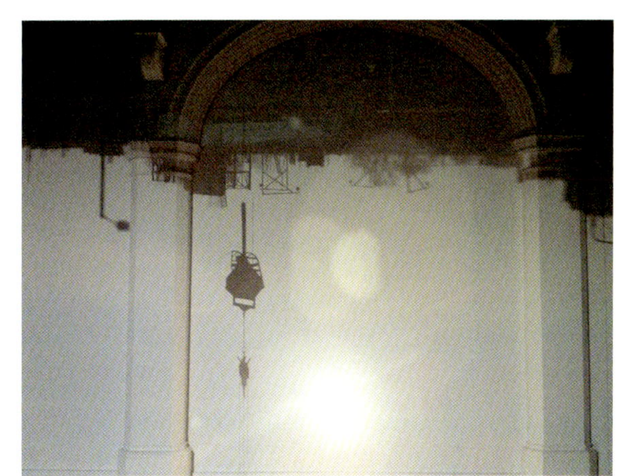

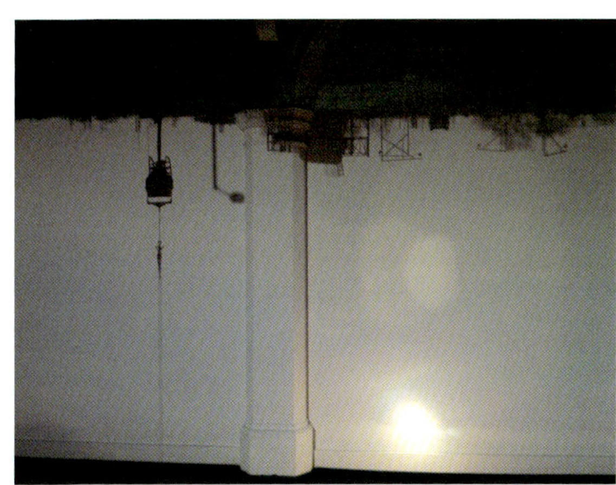

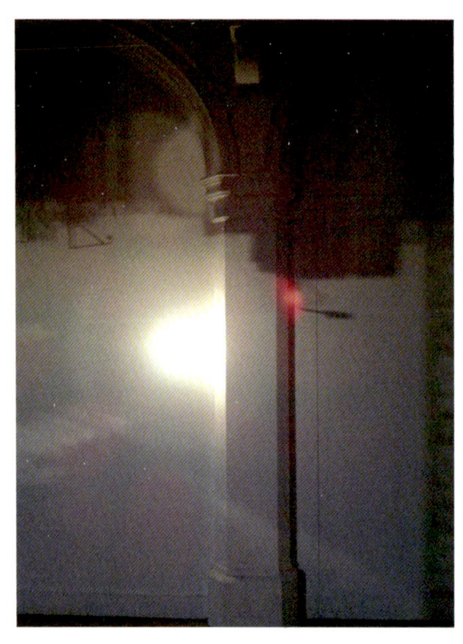 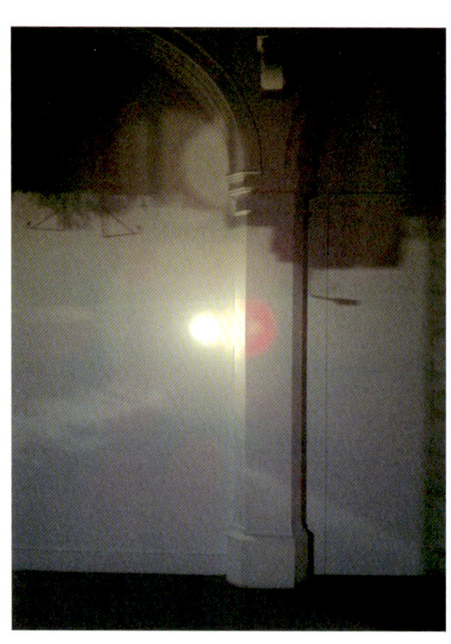

 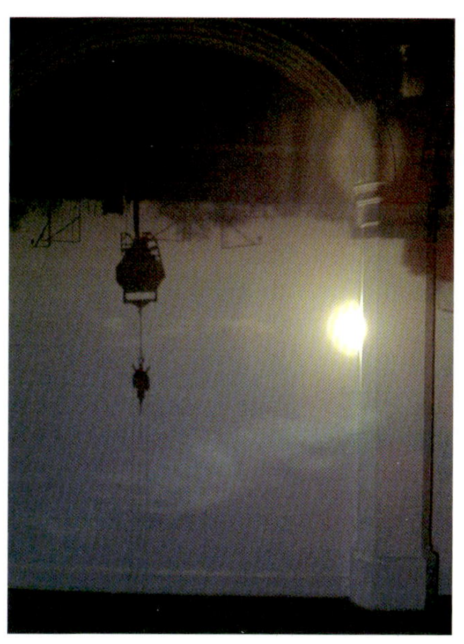

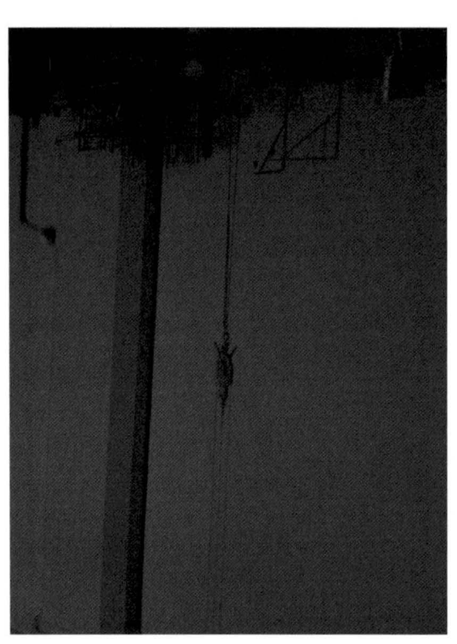

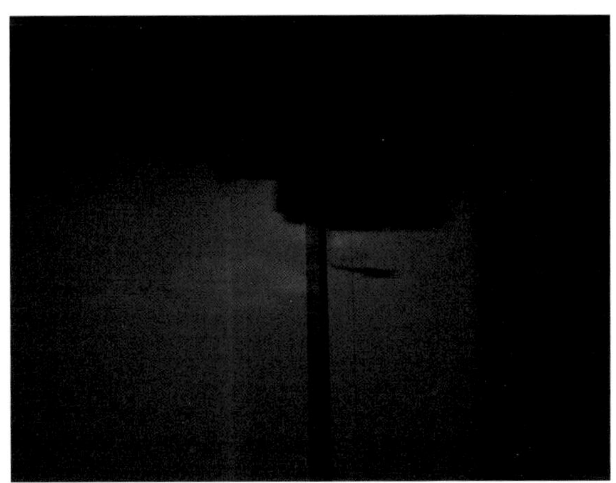

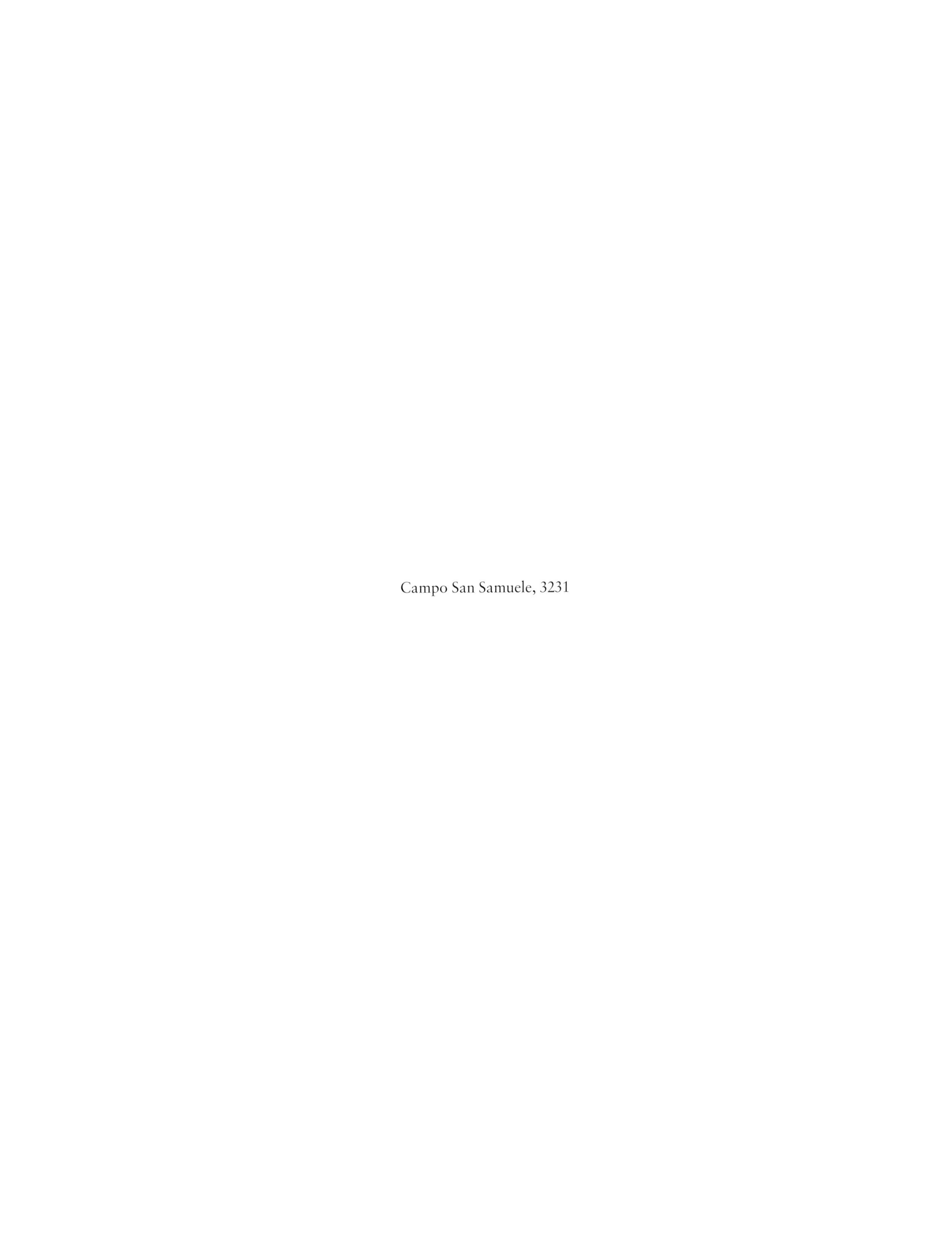

Campo San Samuele, 3231

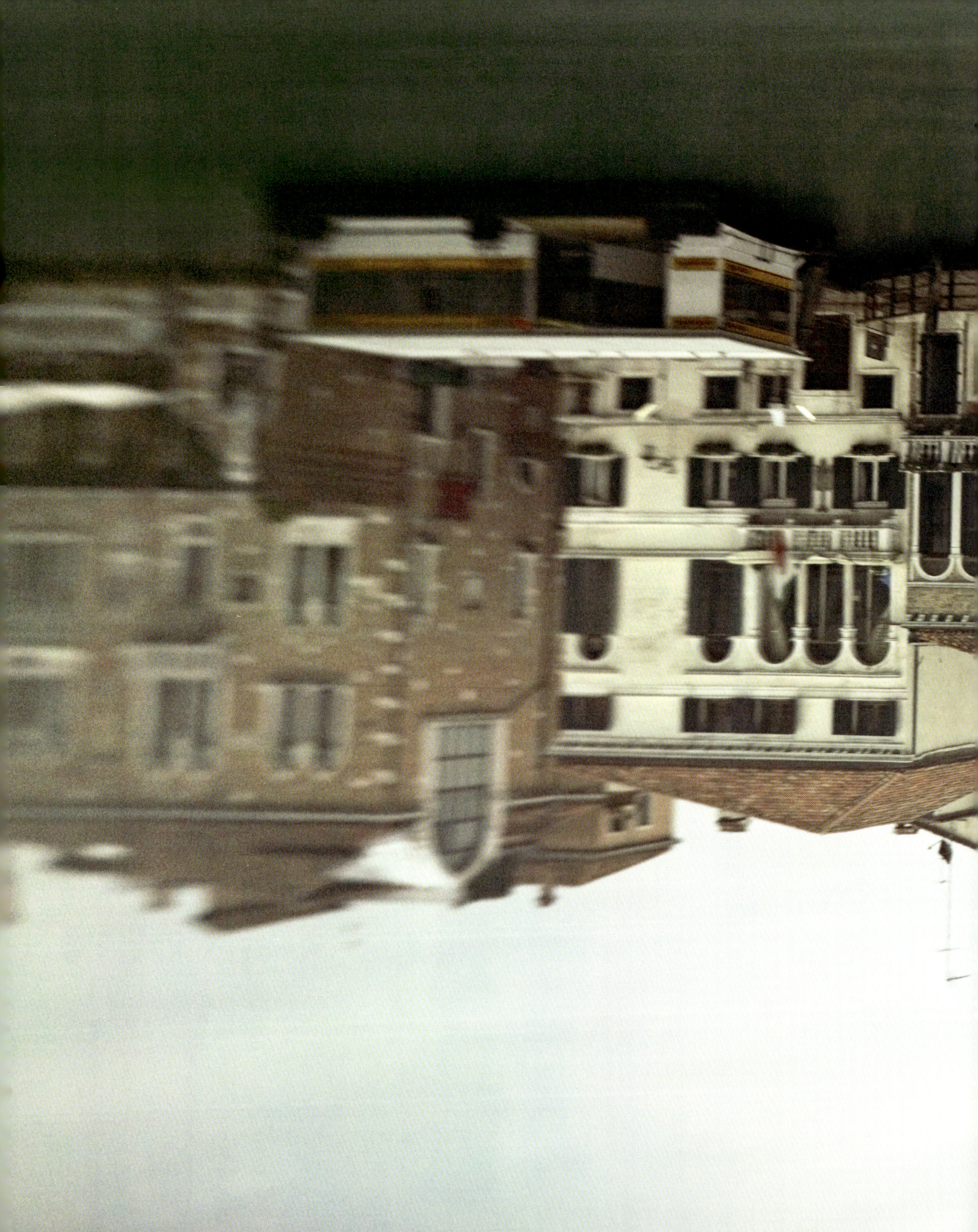

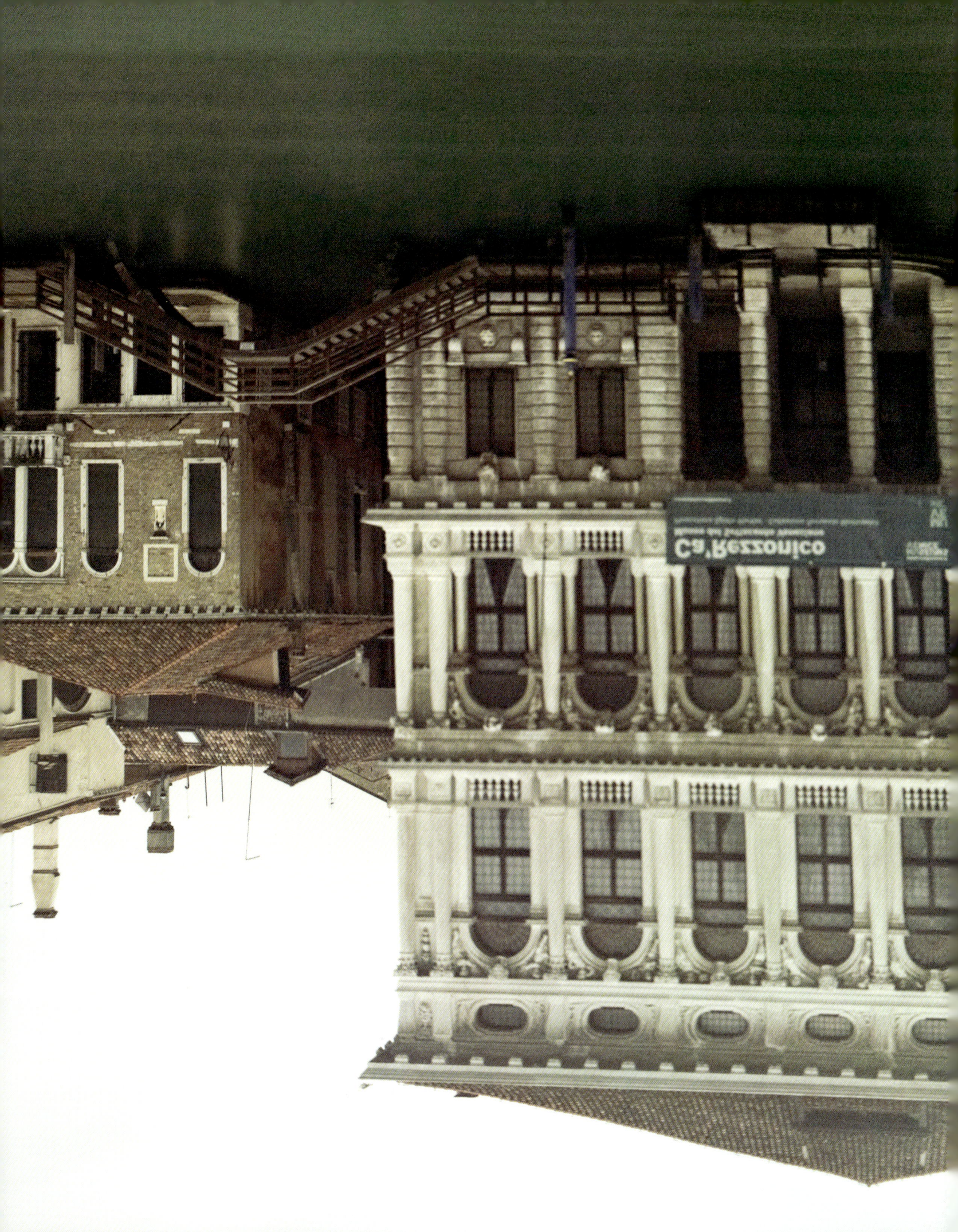

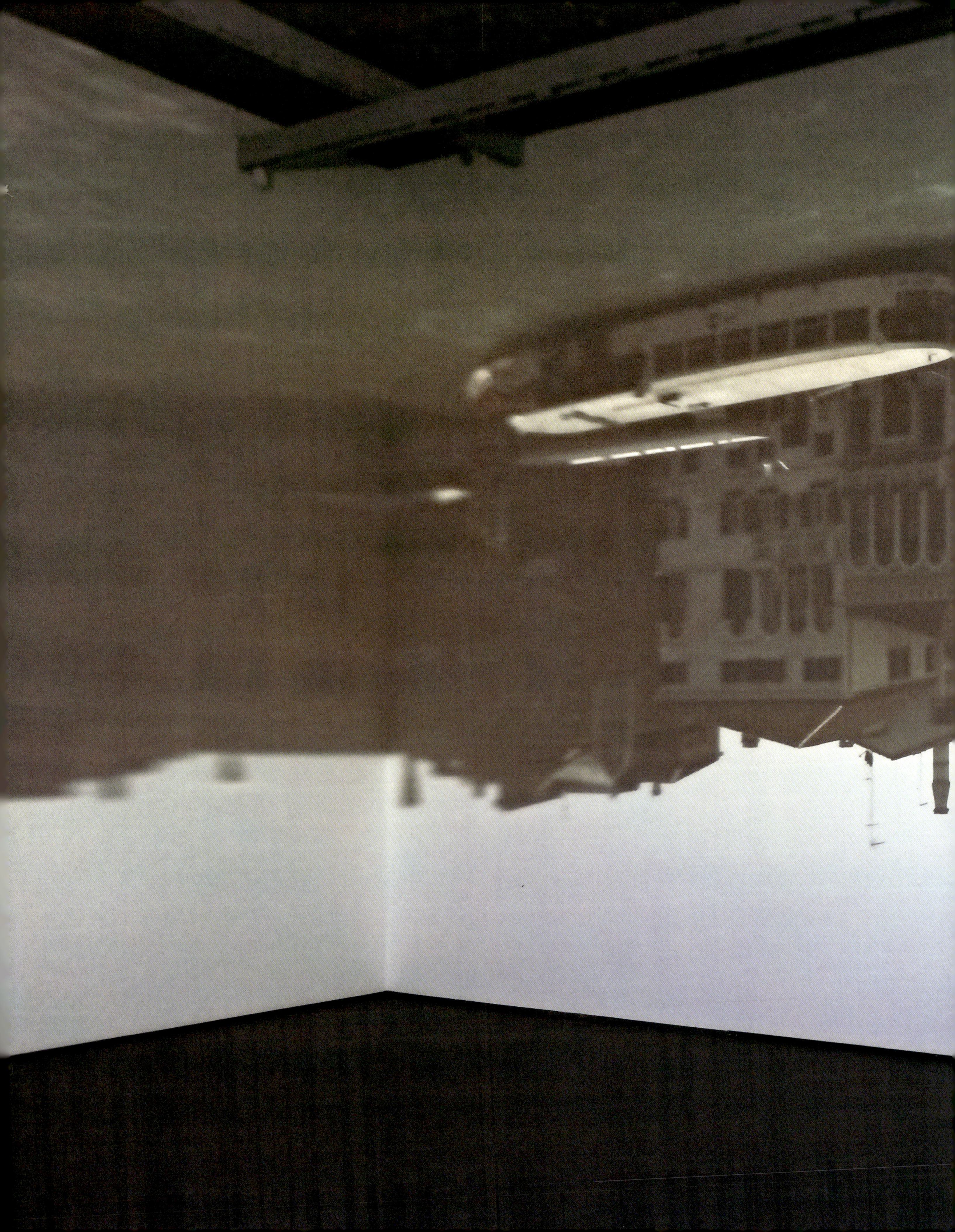

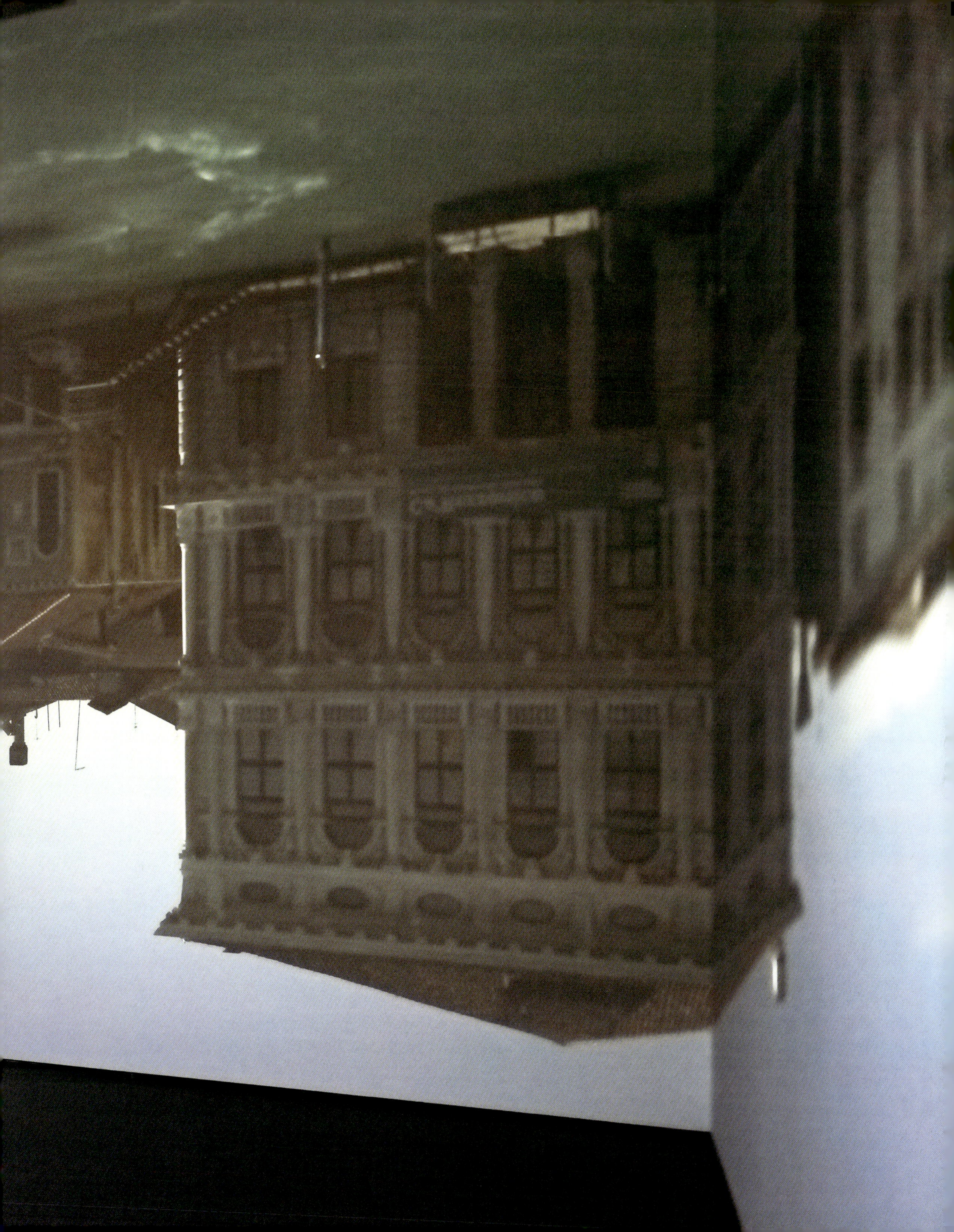

 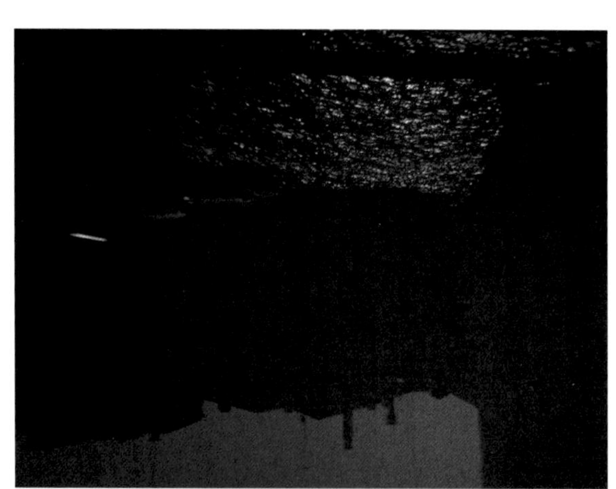

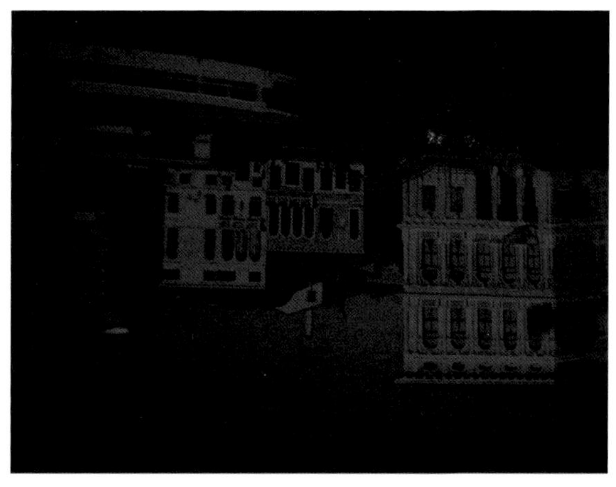

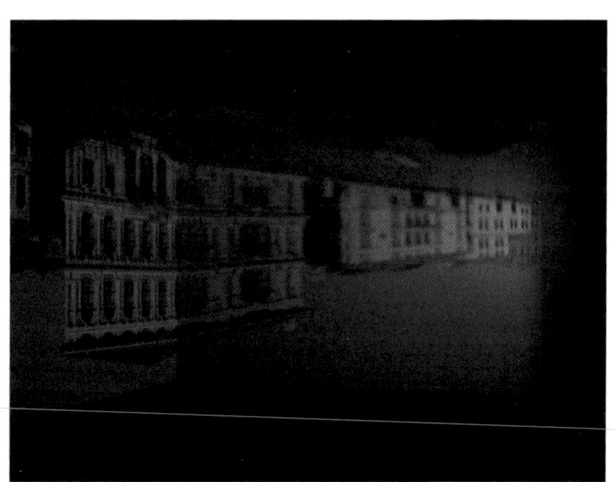

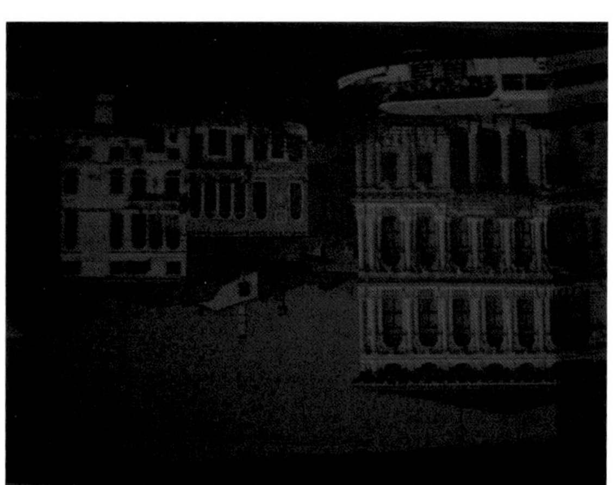

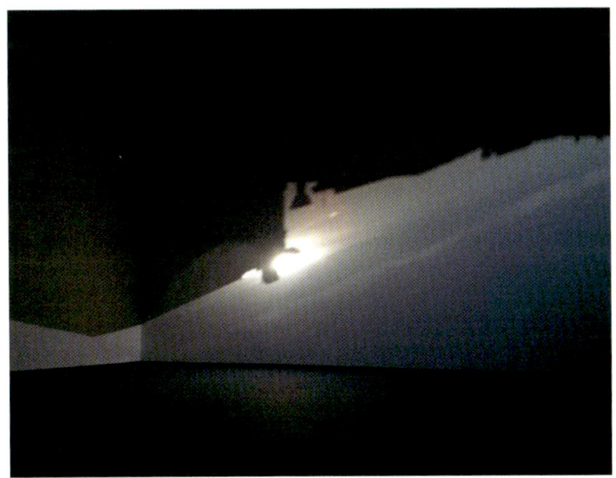
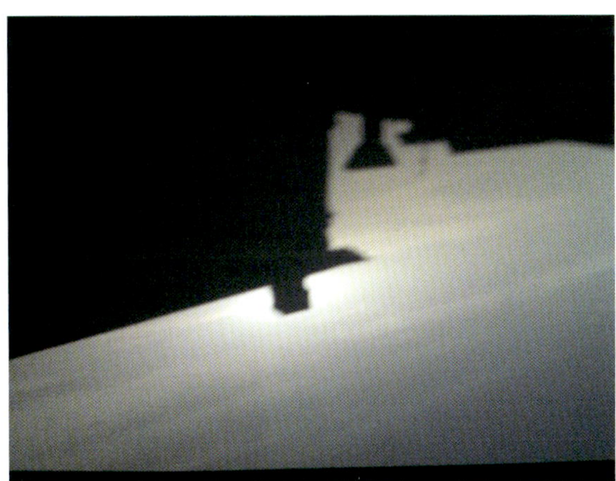

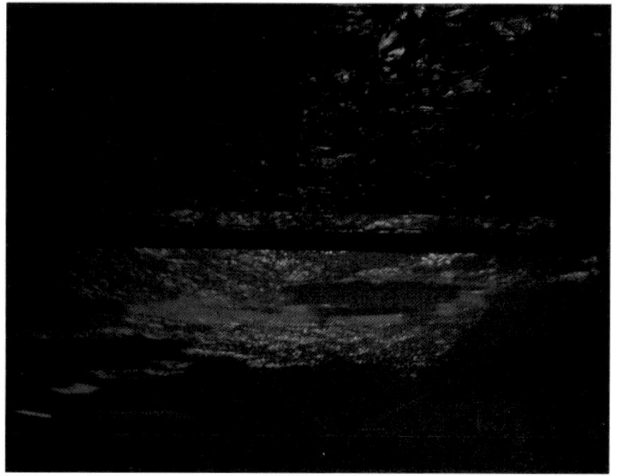

453 West 17th Street

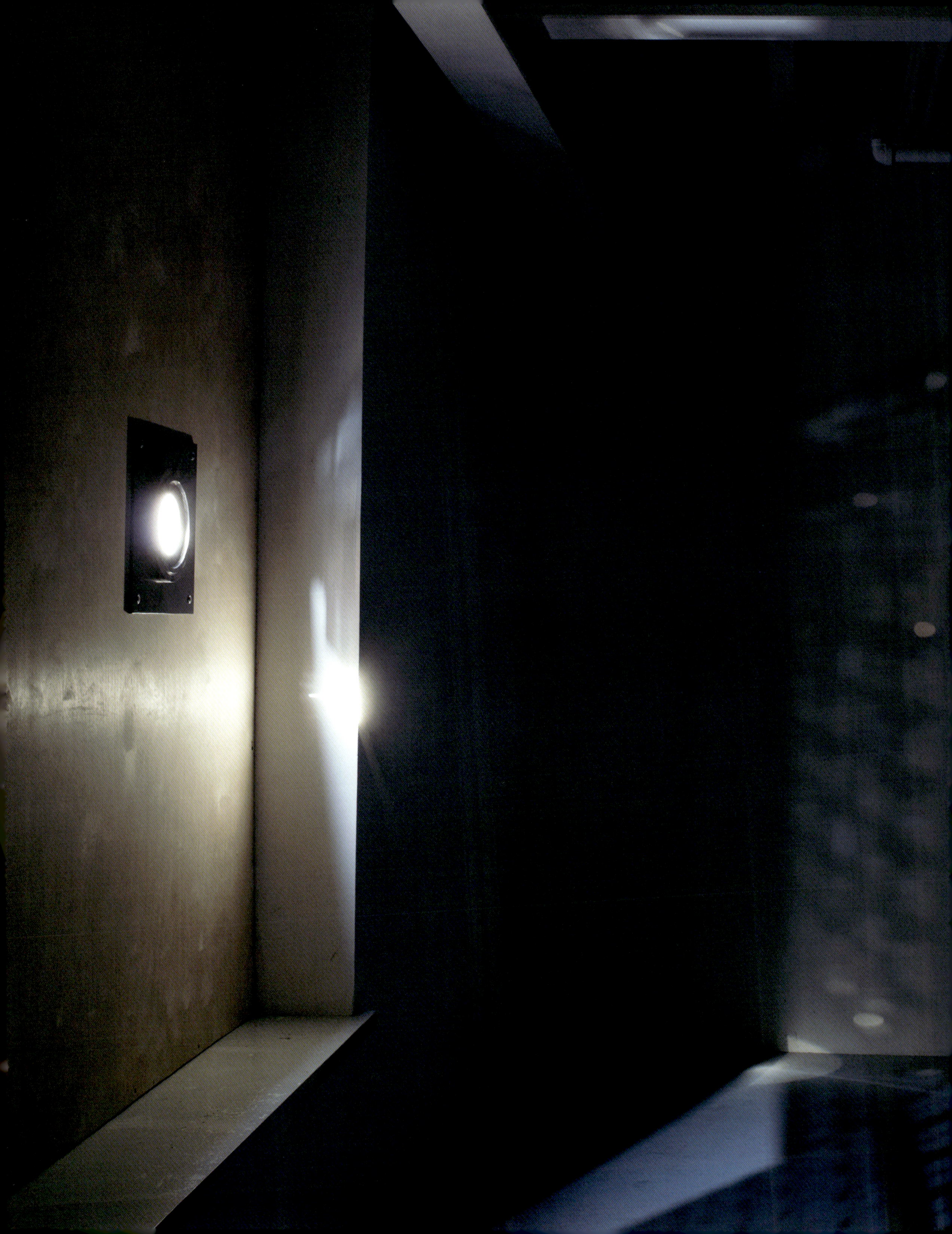

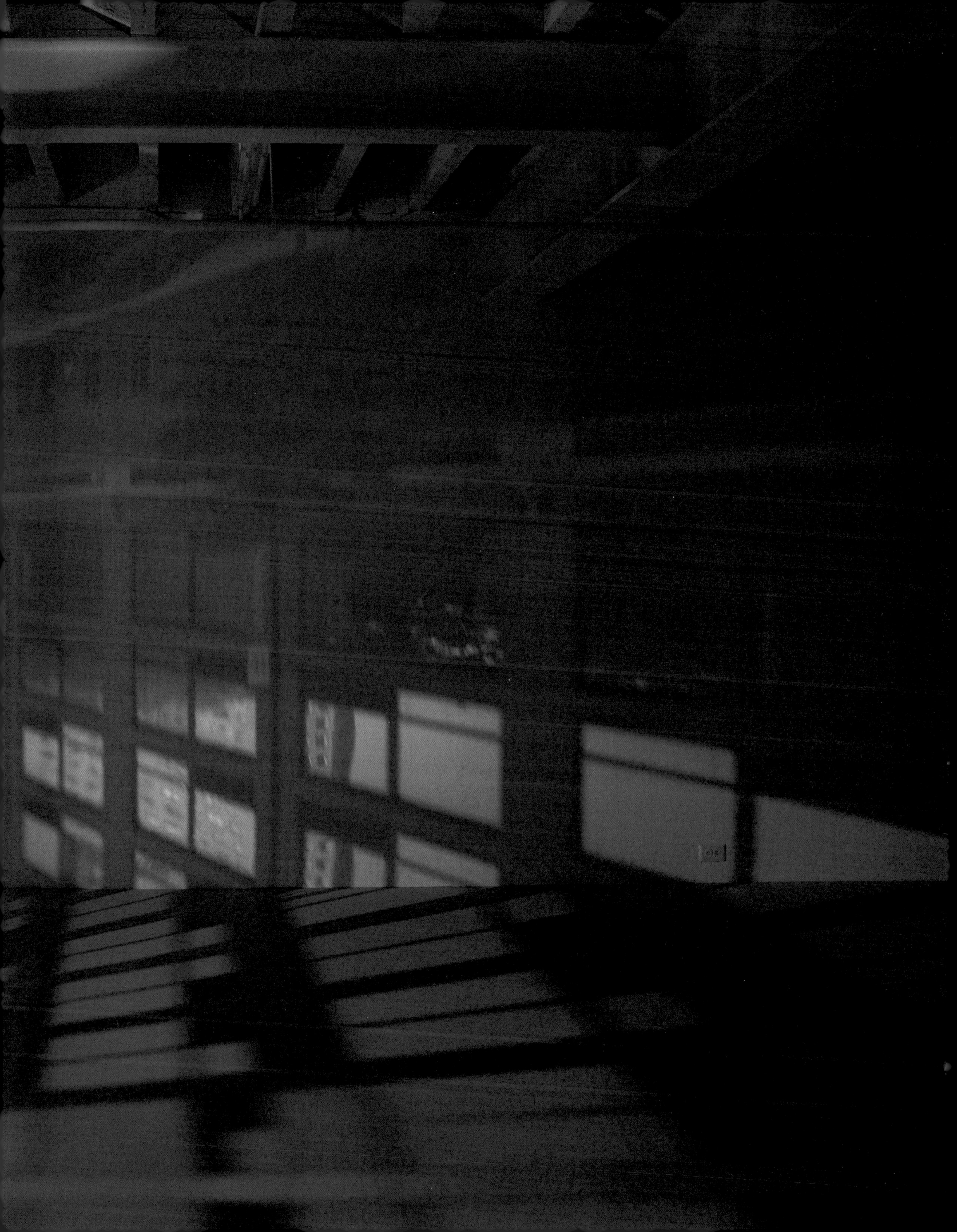

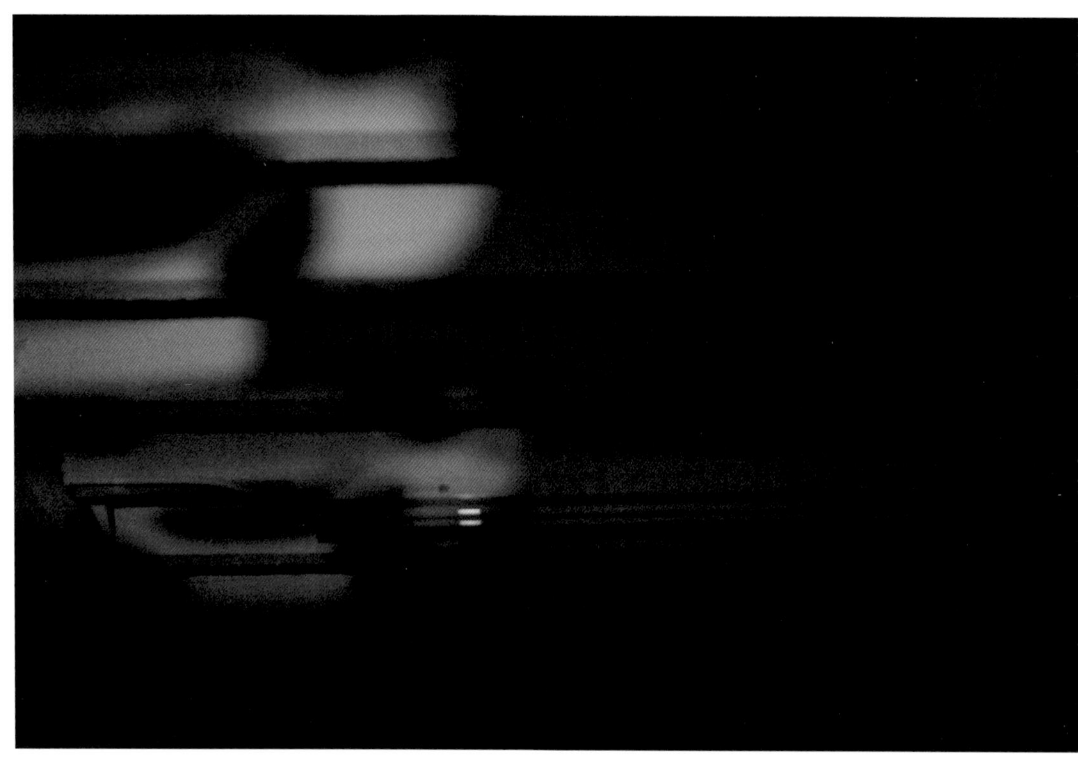

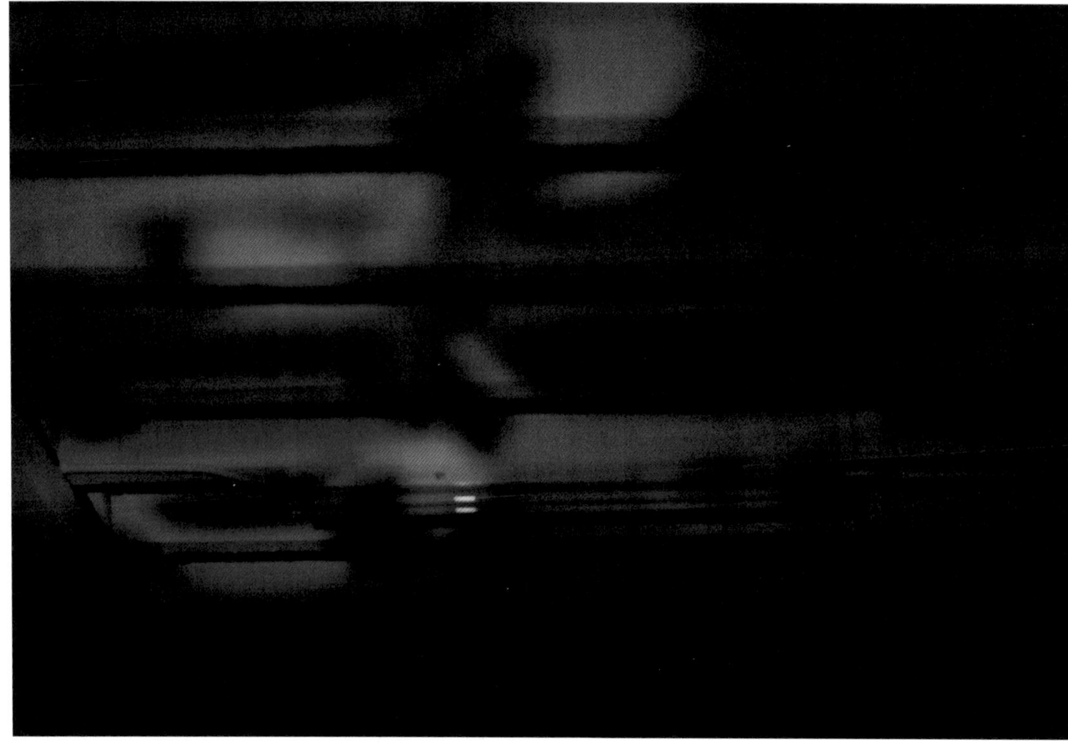

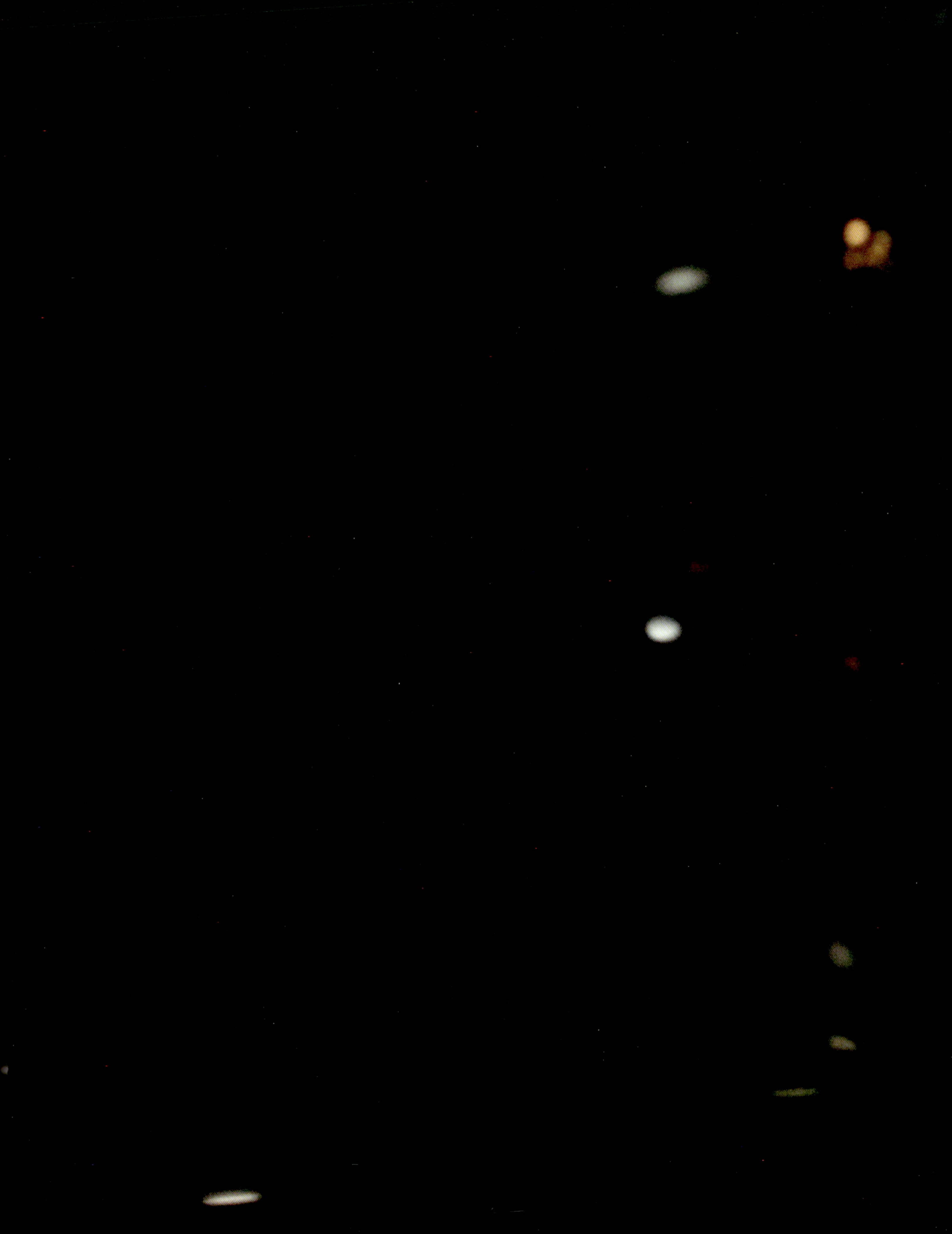

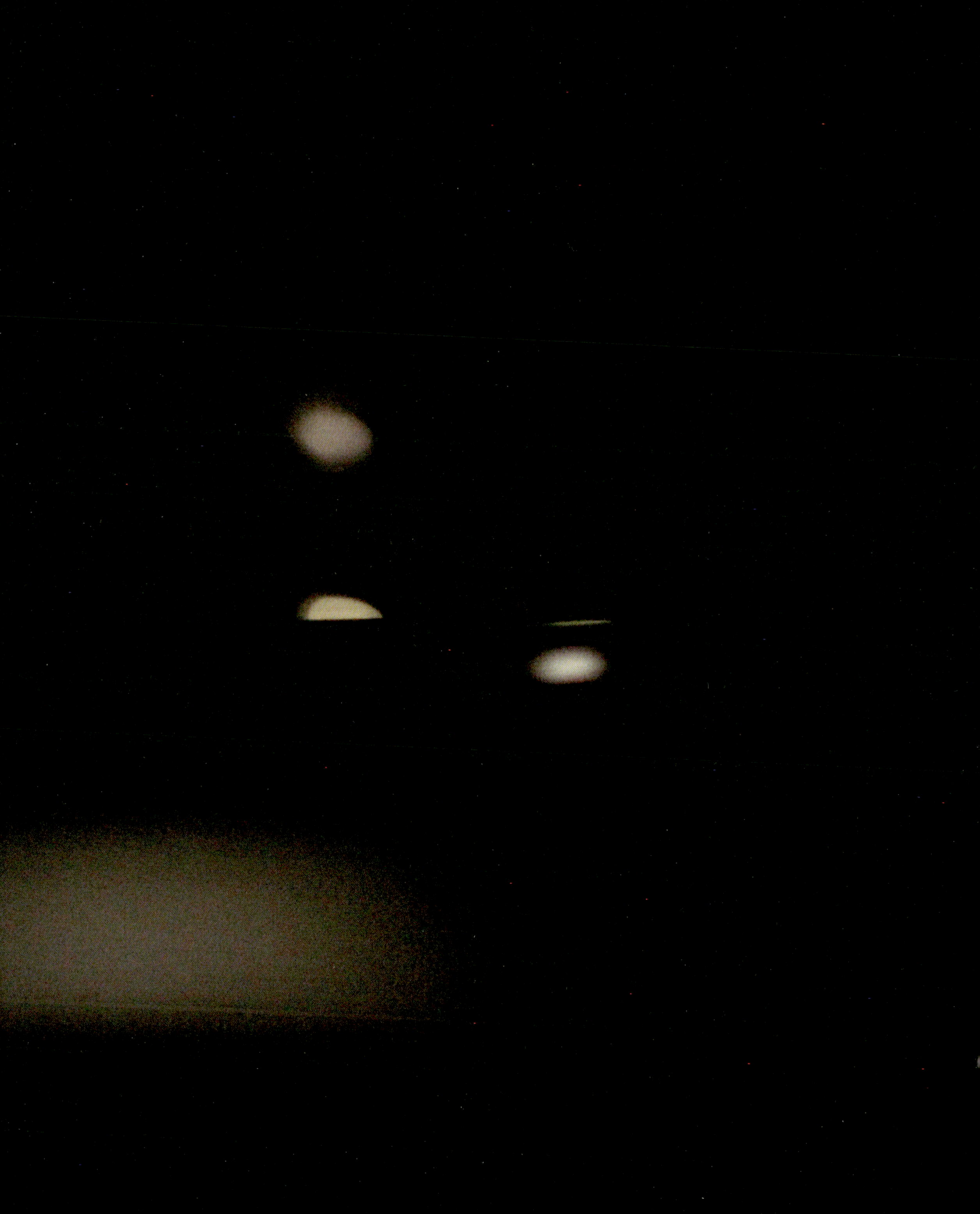

Needleshine

Eileen Myles

In one unforgettable night in my life, I lay on the bed in my tiny apartment with my girlfriend, who was a filmmaker and who at the time was betraying me (or it felt that way at the time), and, lying there, she told me one by one about what each shaking orb in the ceiling in fact represented. I think it was mostly candles and glasses of water. I can't think of what else makes beeping lights pool inside of other pools, all of them overlapping one another to make my ceiling a magic sky, an aquarium of infantile trust. I was awed at her skill at zeroing in on what the real object was that wavered overhead, and I was especially wowed that the occupation of filmmaker had given her a capacity to understand optics in a special way. I am working-class, so I like to see art be of use or have wider, more wiggly applications. I mention betrayal because the poem I tried to make out of this experience was just a repetition of her name, say it was Nineveh. The poem went: "Nineveh told me . . . ," and then I listed what each thing was in the intimate dark, the point finally being that Nineveh was not a trustworthy narrator of much more than just those jars of bouncing light. The poem sucked because I don't think I was able to imply what I felt without ruining it. So I just have it on a scrap of brown paper bag in my papers somewhere, and now someone can know what that was all about when I'm dead.

I'm sort of unteachable. People have always tried to tell me things, show me things, but what I do really like is a tour. It's the finest model I can think of for narrative. Everything that stops and starts is a tour of some kind. On top of a mountain or looking out a window, people love to go: See, *See*, and what they mean is, look at that bridge or up on the mountain, it's like oh . . . let's find our house from up here. Yawn. And I hate in New York when visitors lure me to some tall building and expect *me* to know where things are. What's that bridge. I don't know. I know the world from the inside (alone), and outside it's pretty much some idea of the feeling I'm in: political events, a poem, or my beliefs about this time. I don't know buildings or land—and how to orient myself by saying home is *there*, to better explain where we are standing now, because I know my place so well. I don't. I'm not like that.

So in Turkey this summer, I was sitting on a bench in a town called İznik by a lake. (İznik used to be called Nicaea, home of the Nicene creed, Christianity's most famous prayer, "I believe in God, the Father Almighty . . . creator of all things visible and invisible . . .") I can't resist mentioning here that the Greek word for creed is *sumbolon*, which means something broken into two pieces that when reassembled verifies the person's identity. The word morphed later on into *symbol*. Anyhow, while we were sitting there, John, who has a very good sense of history and location, began naming for me the glittering towns along the distant edges of the lake. I realized quickly that he knew a town by its closeness to the shores of the lake, by its elevation and size and, of course, whether it was to the left or right, corresponding to those north and west and south orientations I never understand unless I'm in New York—a city on a nice 2-D grid, which is one of the things that holds me there, I know.

I suppose, especially at night, there's a childlike feeling of pleasure in knowing that the person you're with knows where you are. I remember adults identifying the fireworks of other towns in the sky on the Fourth of July. Look—there's Braintree, there's Lexington. One of my single favorite spectacles of my life was when I rode in a plane over America, and the pilot telling us that *those* were the Fourth of July firework displays over the Great Salt Lakes, and there's Minnesota, and finally Delaware's display said that we were almost home. It looked like the U.S. was blowing up all night, and I was glad. It was the moment of shock and awe. It seemed right. I was also glad during the bicentennial—1976 when the clouds from the fireworks kept hiding the Statue of Liberty, and the prospect of her being actually gone (maybe the FALN did it, we excitedly hoped) in the midst of the fanfare of America's birthday party was the fantasy of all of my friends. But today, wherever America is, she's still there.

> You are no guest, no stranger.
> On our earth we give birth
> to nothing but ourselves,
> rings linked with rings in a chain.
> —Abraham Sutzkever, "To My Child"

Those are words from a remarkable poet, who wrote them during the Holocaust, when his infant son was condemned to death by the Nazis before he ever lived. No more Jews were to be born in the ghetto in Vilnius, and Sutzkever and his wife's son *was* born, after which a German officer came through the ghetto hospital and put poison on the newborn's lips. Responding to this, Sutzkever's poem suggests he would swallow his son to save him. The idea of a man putting his baby inside, back into the dark of the body as a safe place, feels both potent and timely, as well as the most pithy way I can imagine to bear an unimaginable pain. It's an aspiration of another order. To become something mythic, even female, that could hold the other profoundly.

In Florence, while I was looking at the murals in Santa Maria Novella with an Italian poet, Elisa Biagini, she told me that Purgatory was invented in the twelfth century. Before then, there was only heaven and hell—which were just ways to scare the poor and vulnerable, she said, into being better slaves, essentially, of the church. But then it occurred to some capaciously minded bishop that there could be something in between. Purgatory, a holding tank. And the next thought, of course, was that the church could sell it. These were indulgences, and all of this kicked off Protestantism. But the point was that there always was an in-between space, between good and evil, and by imagining spending time in that in-between space you could now achieve salvation. Waiting. It was a really modern idea.

What is Zoe Leonard achieving by reducing the world to a pinpoint of light that holds everything. What is this social camera of hers, so that the world comes into a room and then in a variety of ways we do too. And she's been repeating this action in particular places around the world, but very much in New York.

We want to be tiny, we want to be small. And at night, well, there's the rub. Zoe invited us all to come one night to Murray Guy in Chelsea, where her camera obscura was installed and we could lie down together on the floor and . . . what. Commune? To hold something. To be a part. I think so. Especially when I think about the sensations I had lying there with people I knew and didn't and most of

them without the identifiers of face and clothes . . . well, I think I might know *that*
voice, but I'm not really sure. And how close should I get? How close to anyone.
What if I step on someone here. Or someone steps on me. And my glasses. I left
them on the floor. Where are they? If someone steps on my glasses . . . The night
will be endless. Pillows were offered, shoved in my direction, and I wondered if a
pillow meant I was special or someone else just left, or if I was old. Or, again, was
it a way of pulling me close. Were all the pillows together. Who were those people
sitting against the wall. When did they go. When we settled in, which was instanta-
neous and then long (because no one could watch my growing comfortable or not.
Like meditation or writing or prayer, my entire process was my own), I don't know
how long I lay in the darkness that grew lighter. Yes, darkness changes and grows
features. Darkness was getting born. And so were we. I saw a stripe of conveyance.
A street. And it had layers of surrounding stripes, ripples in a multitude of tones,
many streets. And they were pulsing and changing as people opened doors, and a ray
of light changed the shape of it all. That's someone on a bike. There's a car. Really.
Yes, that's a car. Each time a new group formed and changed within the room and
the room itself and the same conclusions were arrived at and new ones were devel-
oped. Yes, it's a darkroom, duh. Some people were just very good at guessing. Or
knowing. Some cared. I didn't. I mean, I cared in my way, I cared about everything.
I liked being in the room. I've heard lately about composers who are having special concerts in the dark. Not on the esplanade but the dark inside a new collective
space. Why? Is this sculpture, is this activism. Is it poetry. *Oui.* Cause Purgatory
must exist in our time in a gray space where the meanings are unclear, except for the
fact that we have incremental amounts of time and we are spending some of it inside
now and together. Does anyone know about us and our listening parties and our
seeing events. Our unplugged events. Our readings. How do we relate to the rooms
of people all over the world who are simply living, not by choice, without power.
Or sporadically. We lie here in our unspecial, shared blindness in which the night is
invented again in opposition to out there and because of it.

I've read that there weren't any Dark Ages really. I think they were constructed
to springboard the Enlightenment, which we don't so much believe in now. It didn't
suddenly get light, and everything in the darkness before was bad and needed to
die. Who were killed in the short and long cultural nights, when everyone could see
but someone right in front of you was saying no this isn't happening here, what you
think you are seeing isn't true. But it is. Sutzkever went a few years later to Vilnius
to a space, a tiny space under a roof, where all he had was a pinhole of light, and
in that crevice he, unlike his son, did survive the war, and years later he returned to
that ghetto and that nook where he hid. He wrote:

Liberated, when I returned
To my hiding place—
In the same needleshine I saw,
Quivering in the ray of dust,
A familiar figure. I could swear:
I it was. And am. And shall remain,

Strung on a string of dust
With the same needle.
        —Abraham Sutzkever, "Needleshine"

We went out and had dinner afterward. Did you join us. It was fun. We should do this more. Yeah, we should see each other more often. I remember the young Zoe Leonard, when she showed slides of her girlfriend, Simone, at some one-night lesbian club. Her photos were devotional. Simone *was* beautiful. She worked at Café Orlin, and everyone said who's she. She was Zoe's, and she was her first subject, or her photography was her love. Darkrooms to walls to darkened rooms. Pinups of beauty. Nothing to see, but the city made tiny and us. Only our adorable syntax, our capacity to huddle in darkness, our love, a litter of friends, silent, laughing and waiting. This is her generous portrait now.

I it was. And am. And shall remain,
Strung on a string of dust
With the same needle.
        —Abraham Sutzkever, "Needleshine"

Translation of Abraham Sutzkever's poem "Needleshine" by Barbara and Benjamin Harshav; translation of "To My Child" by Lee Sharkey and Joshua Waletzky

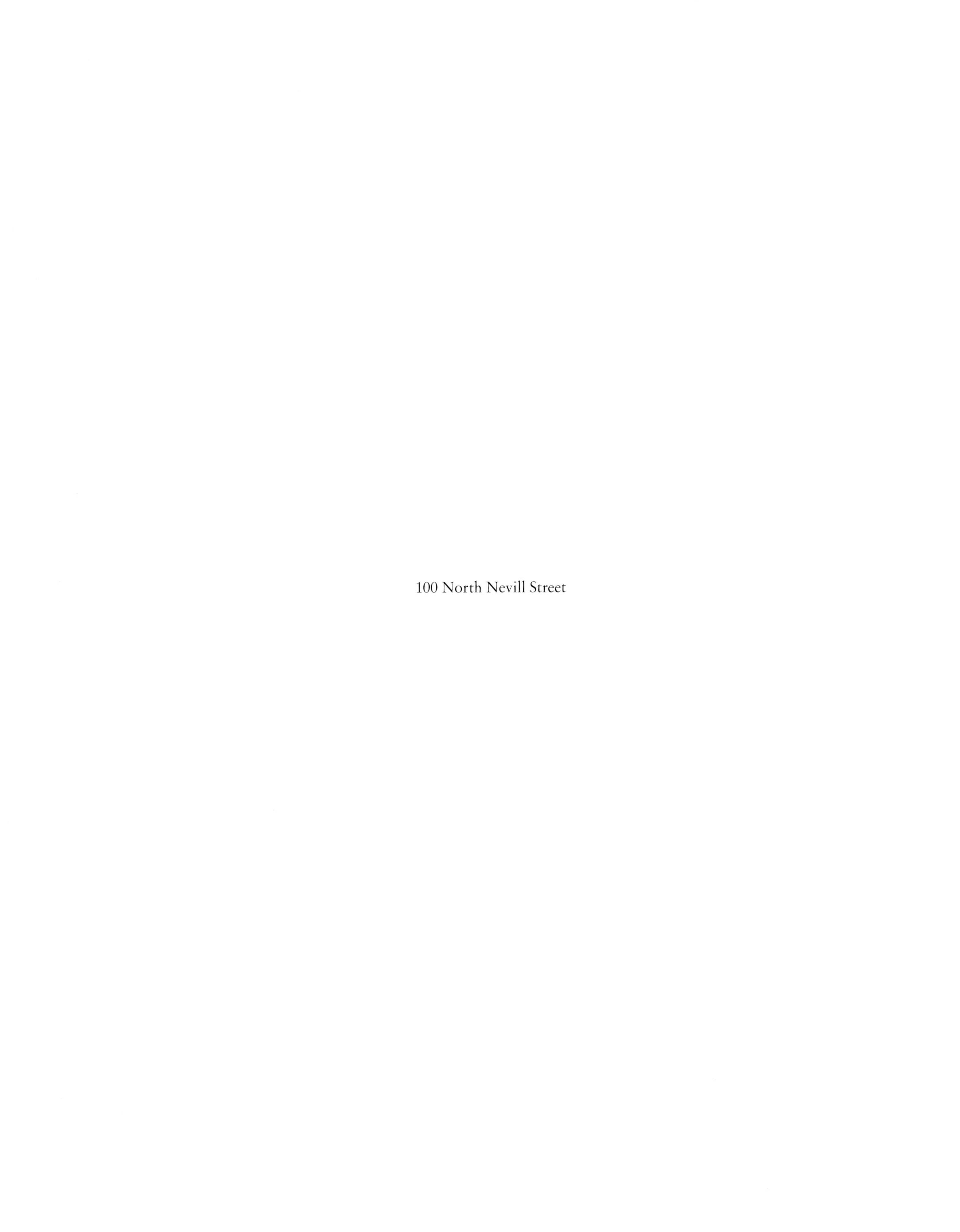
100 North Nevill Street

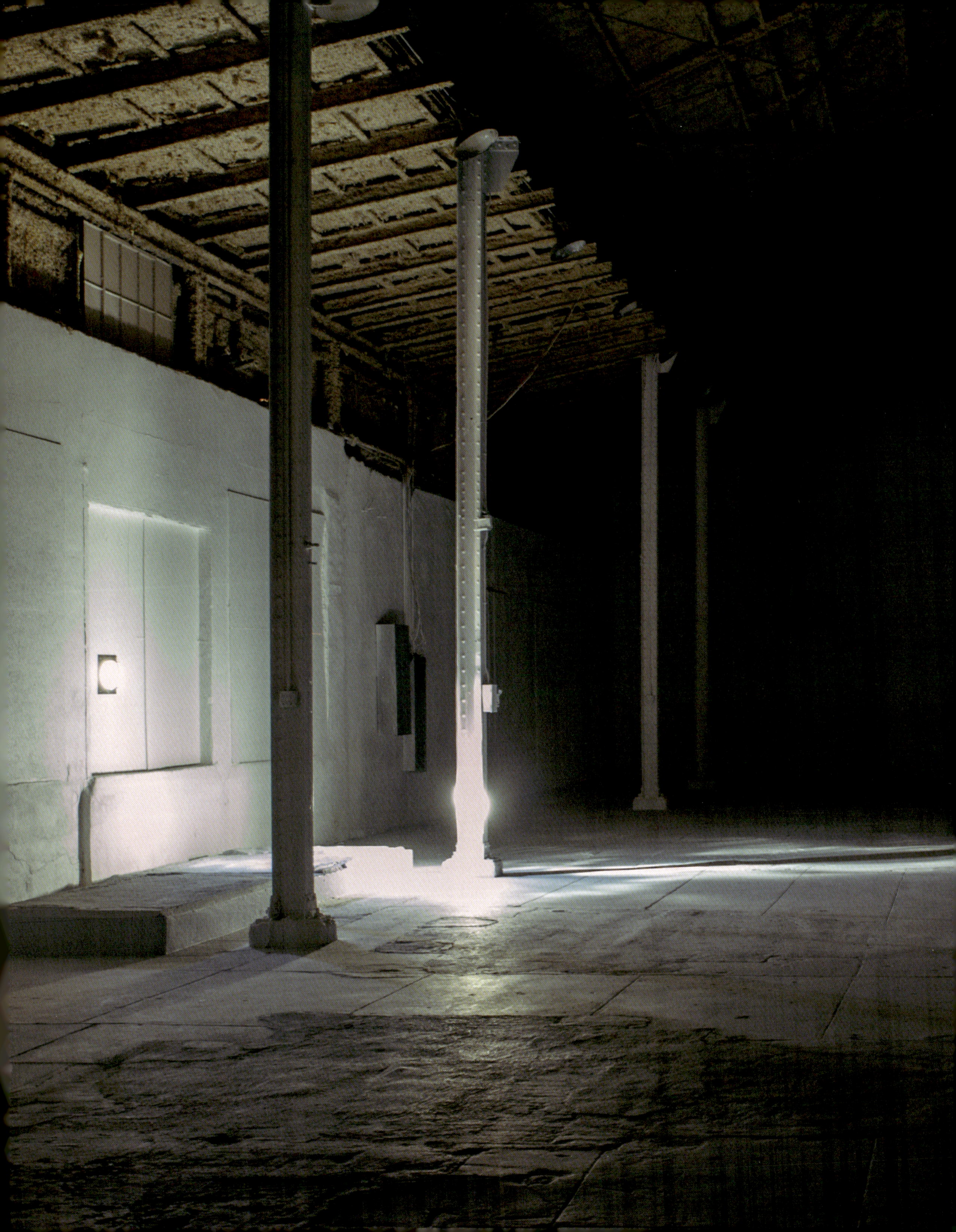

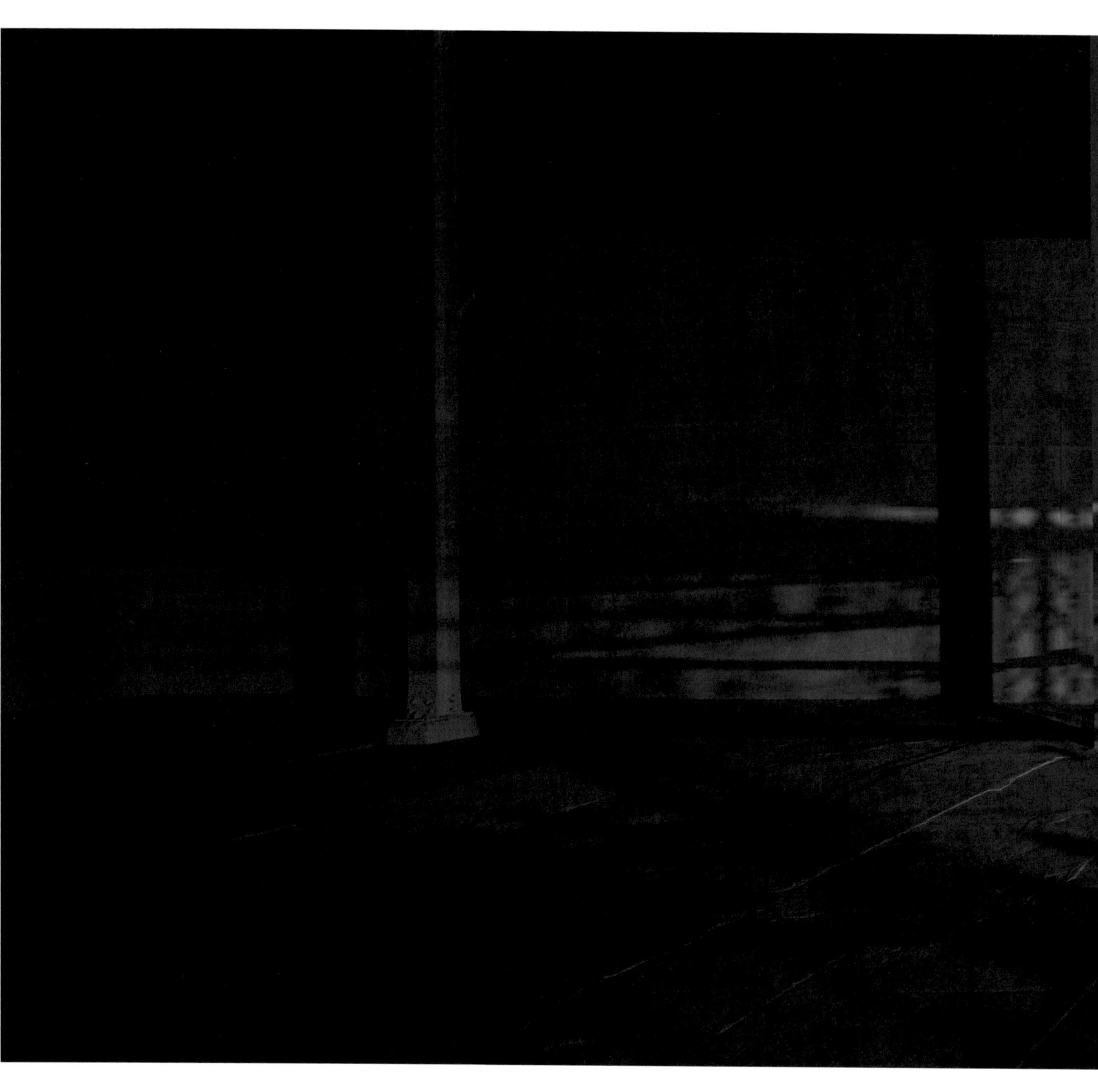

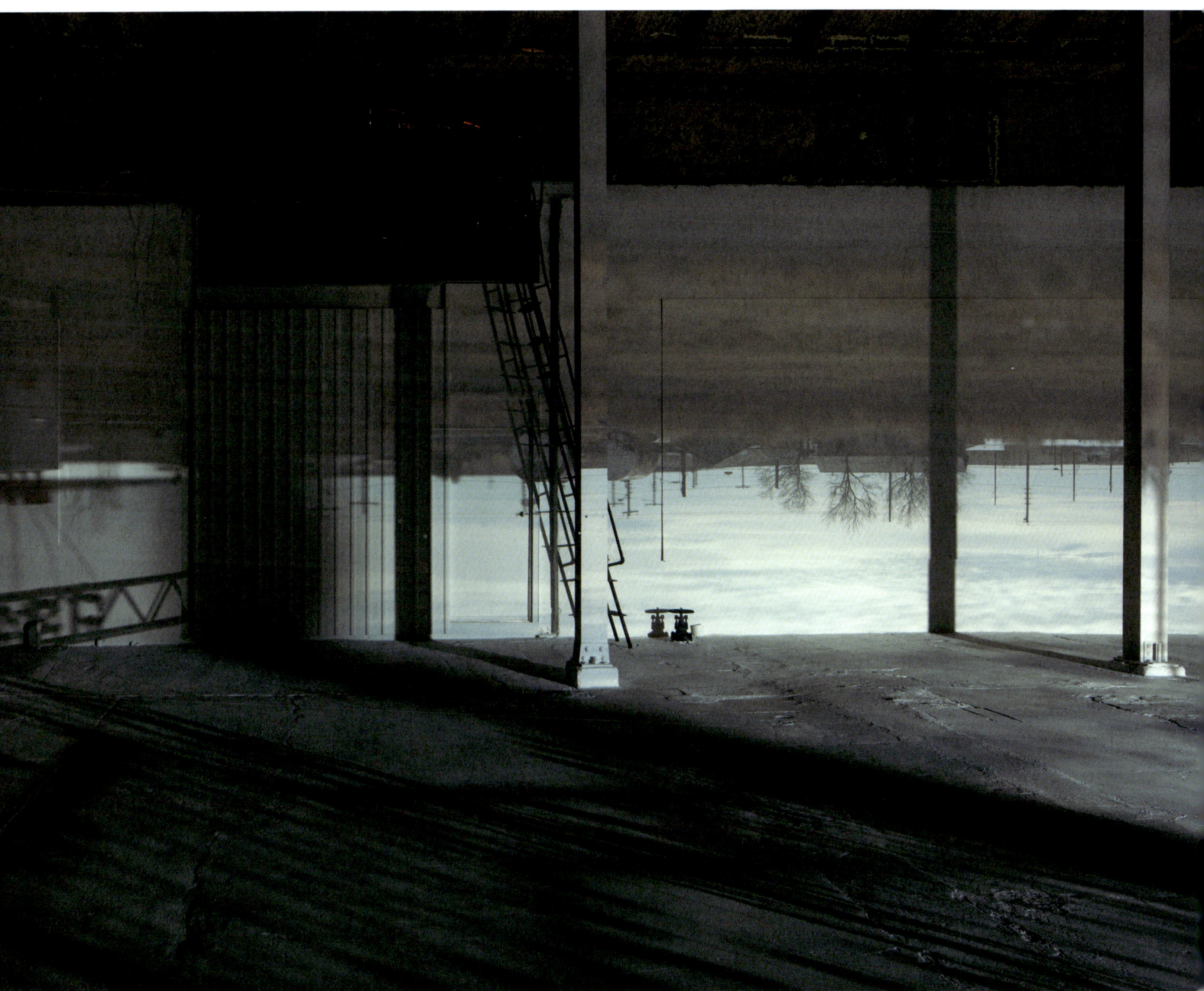

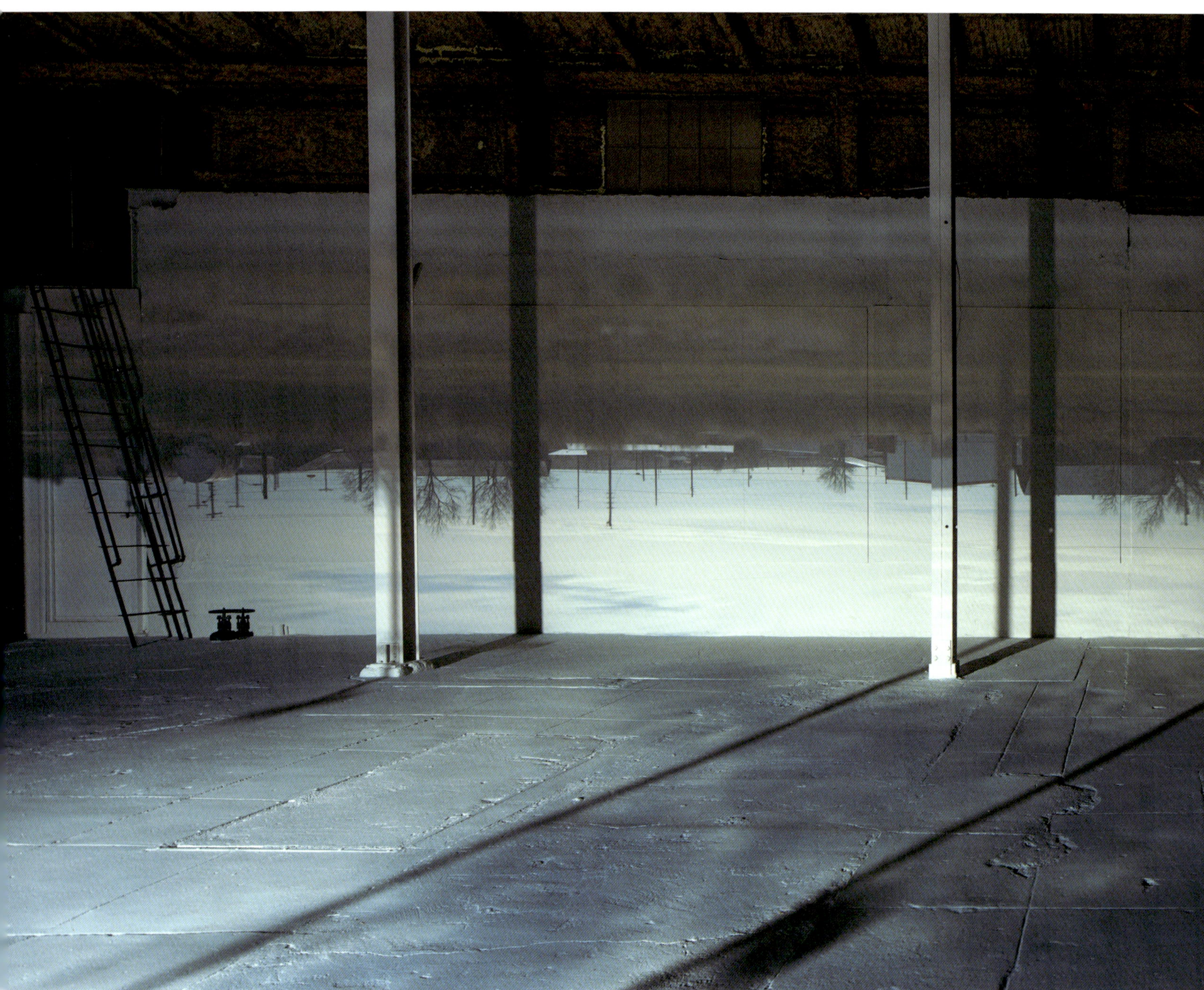

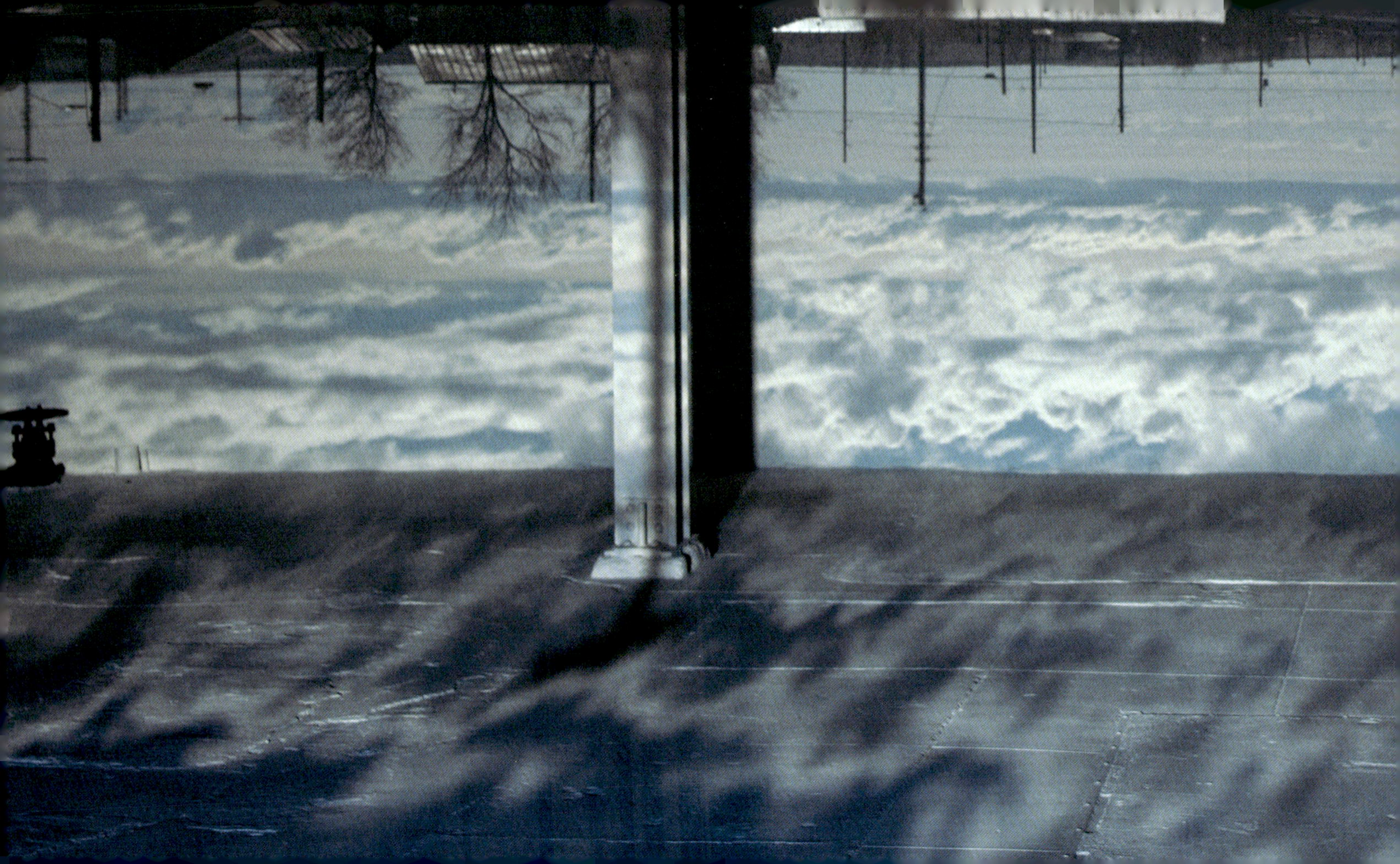

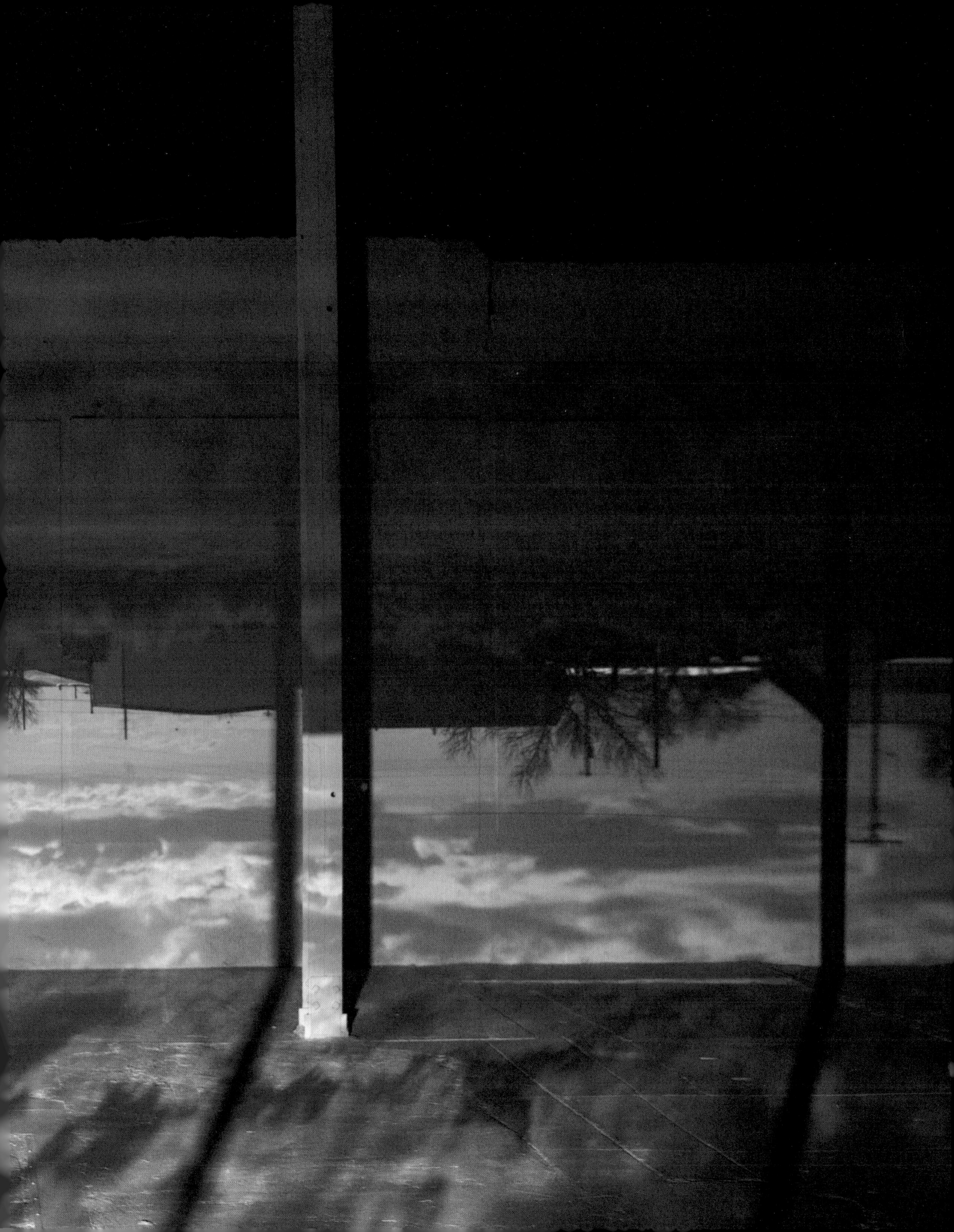

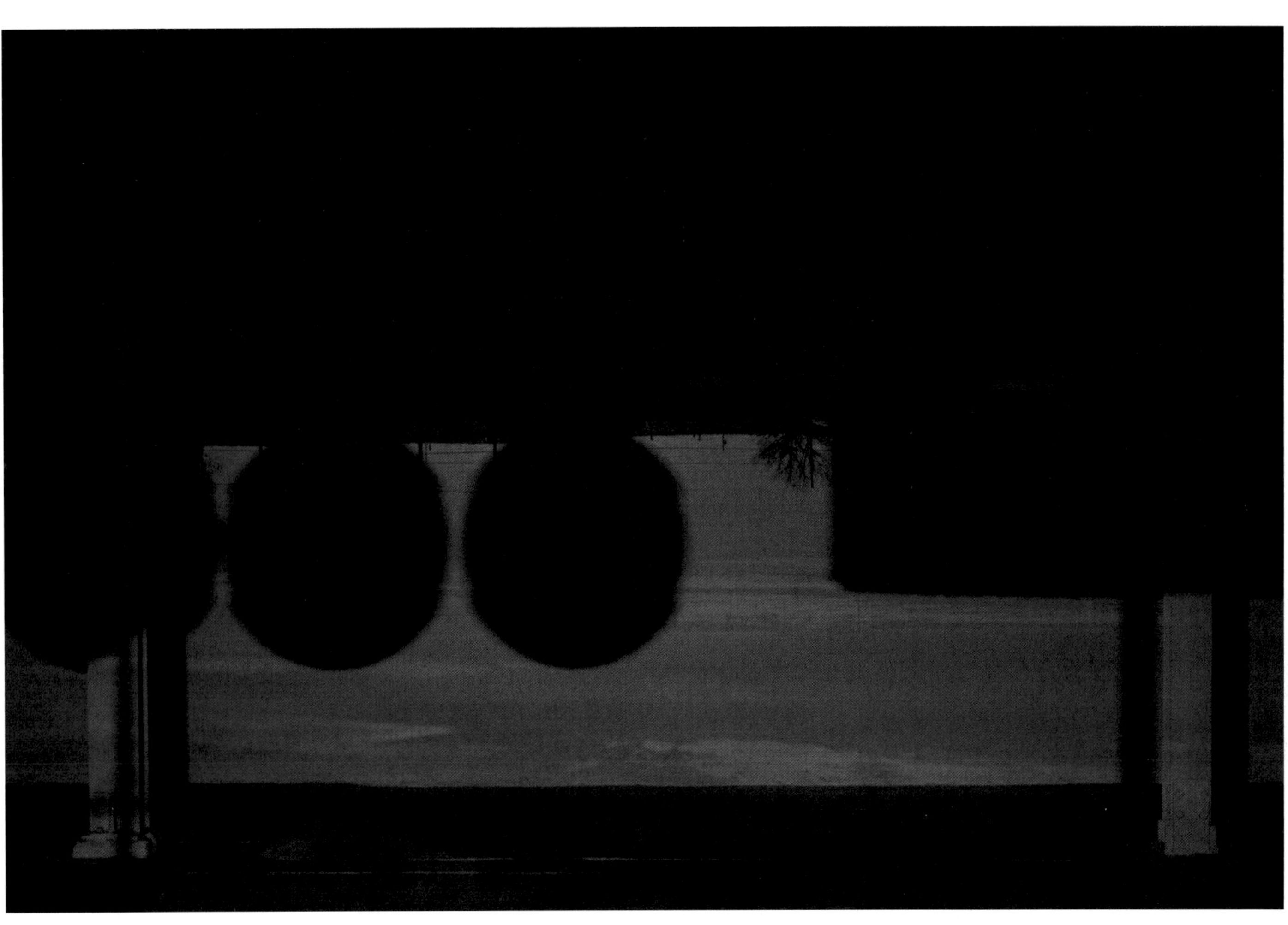

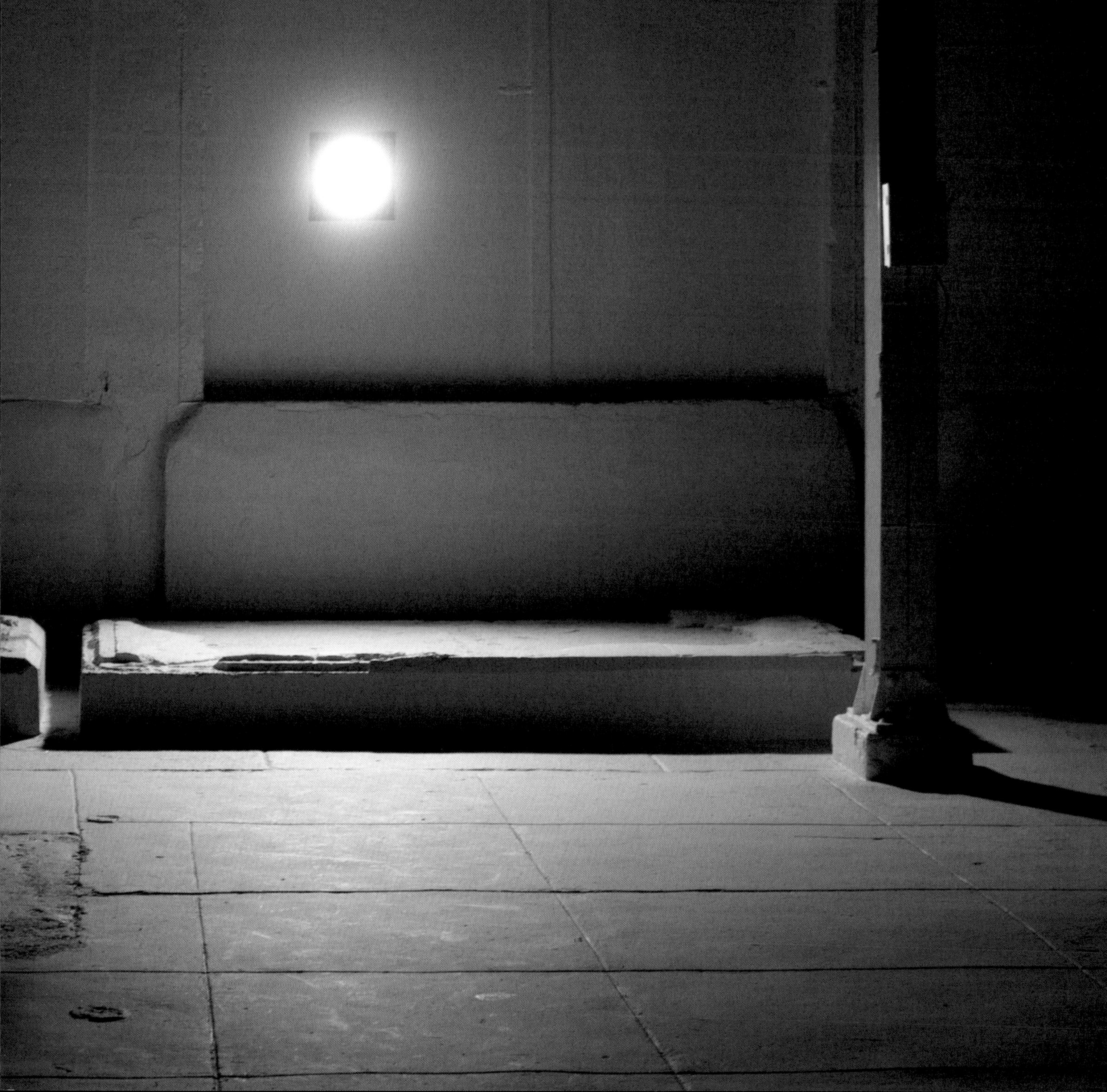

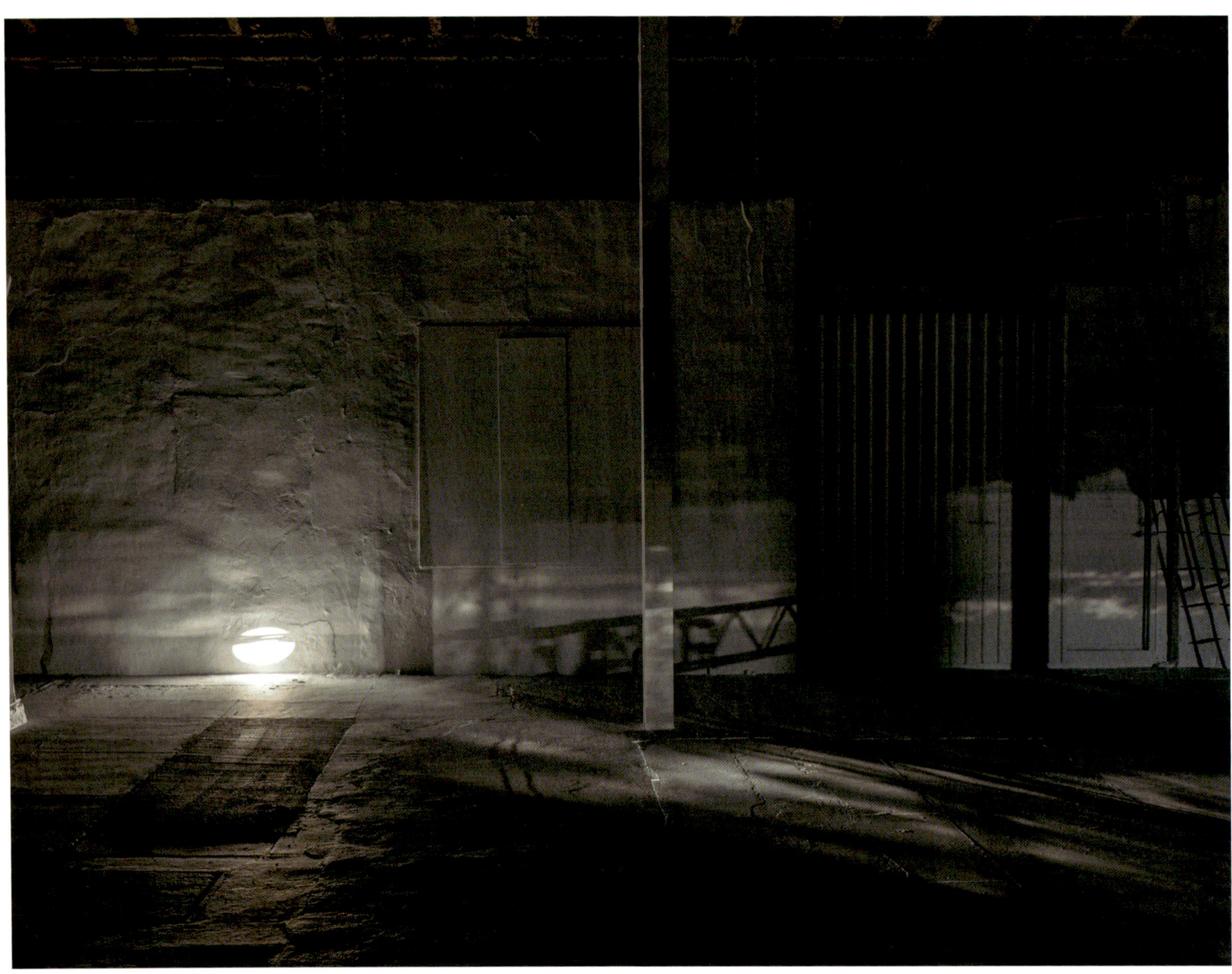

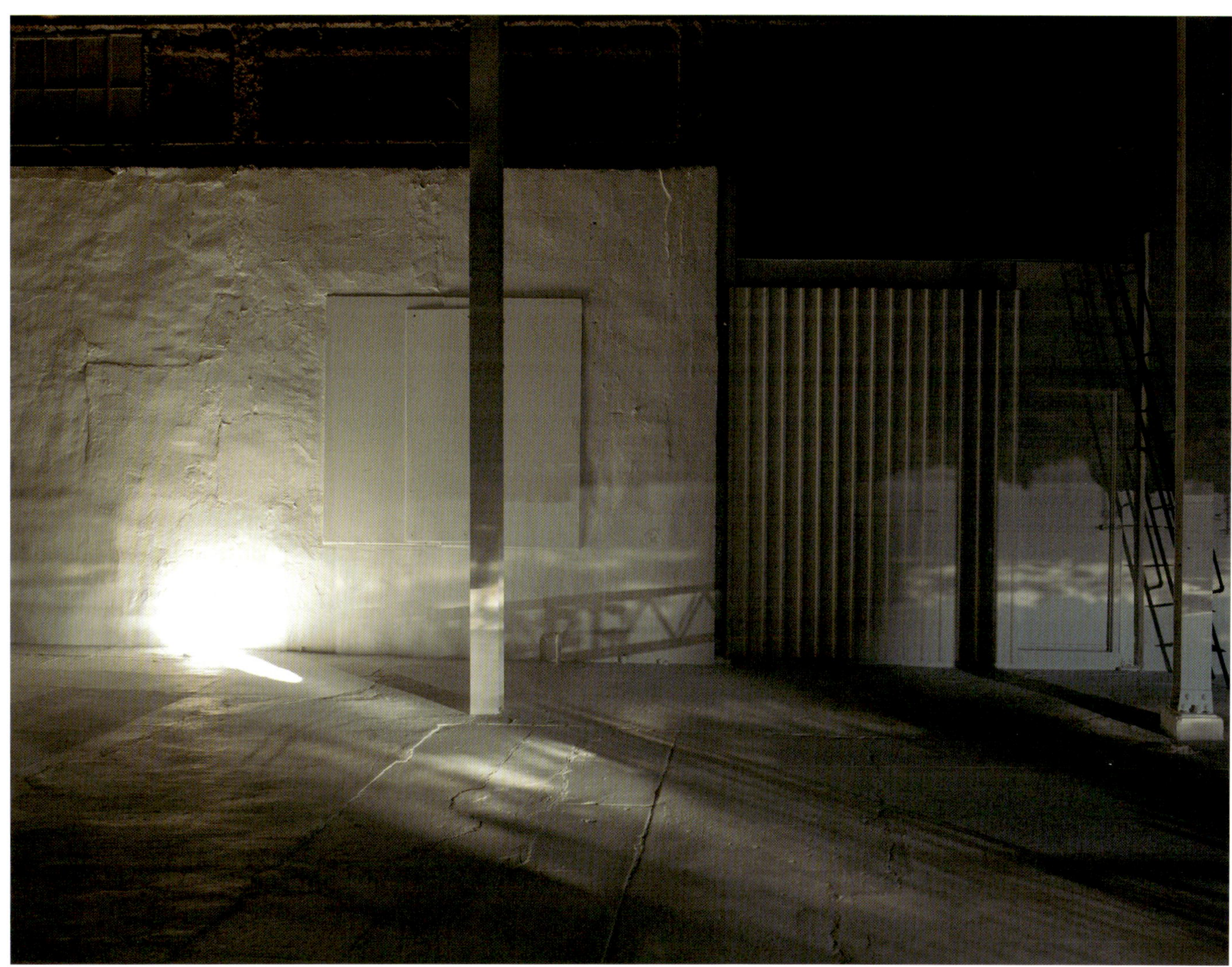

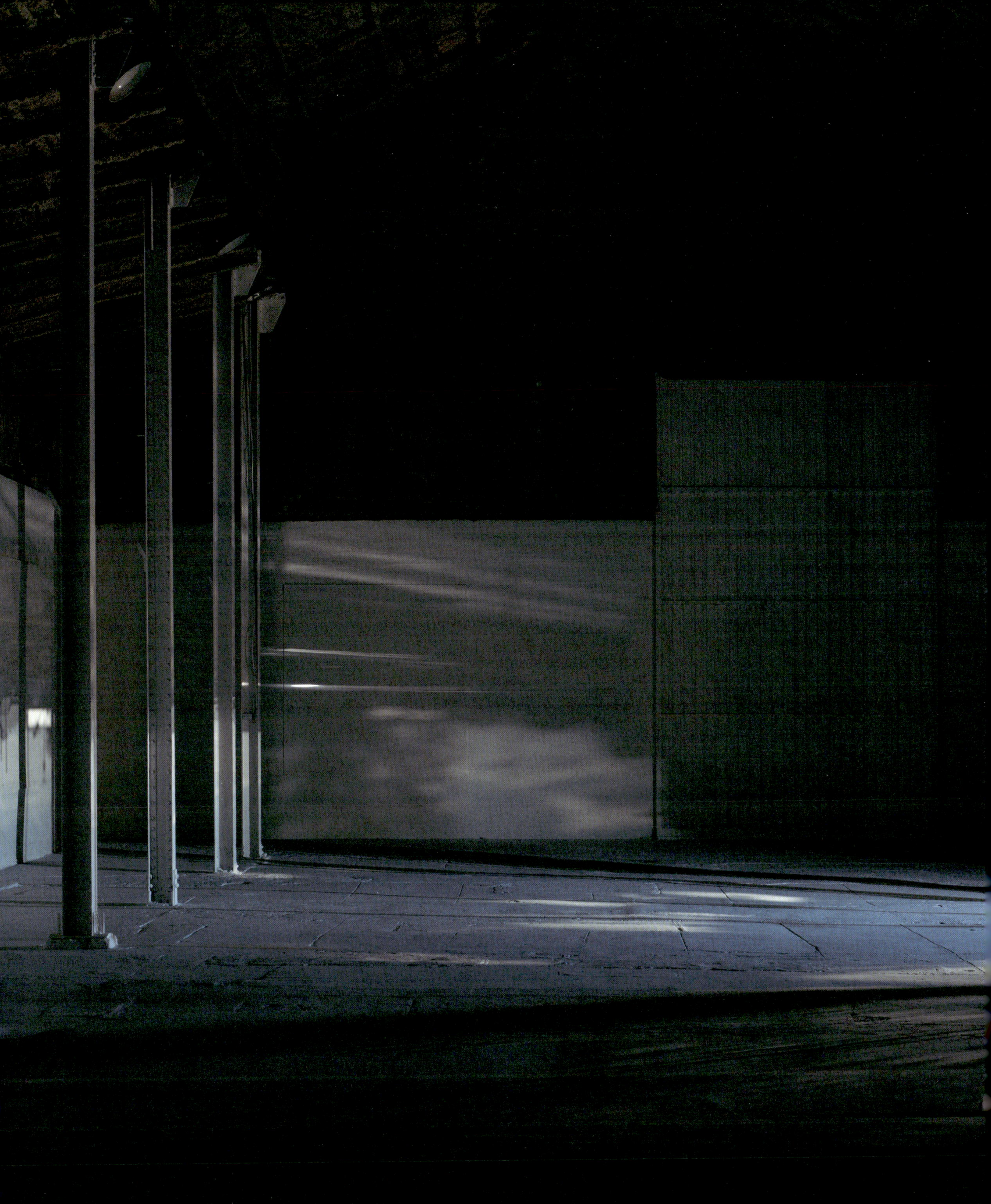

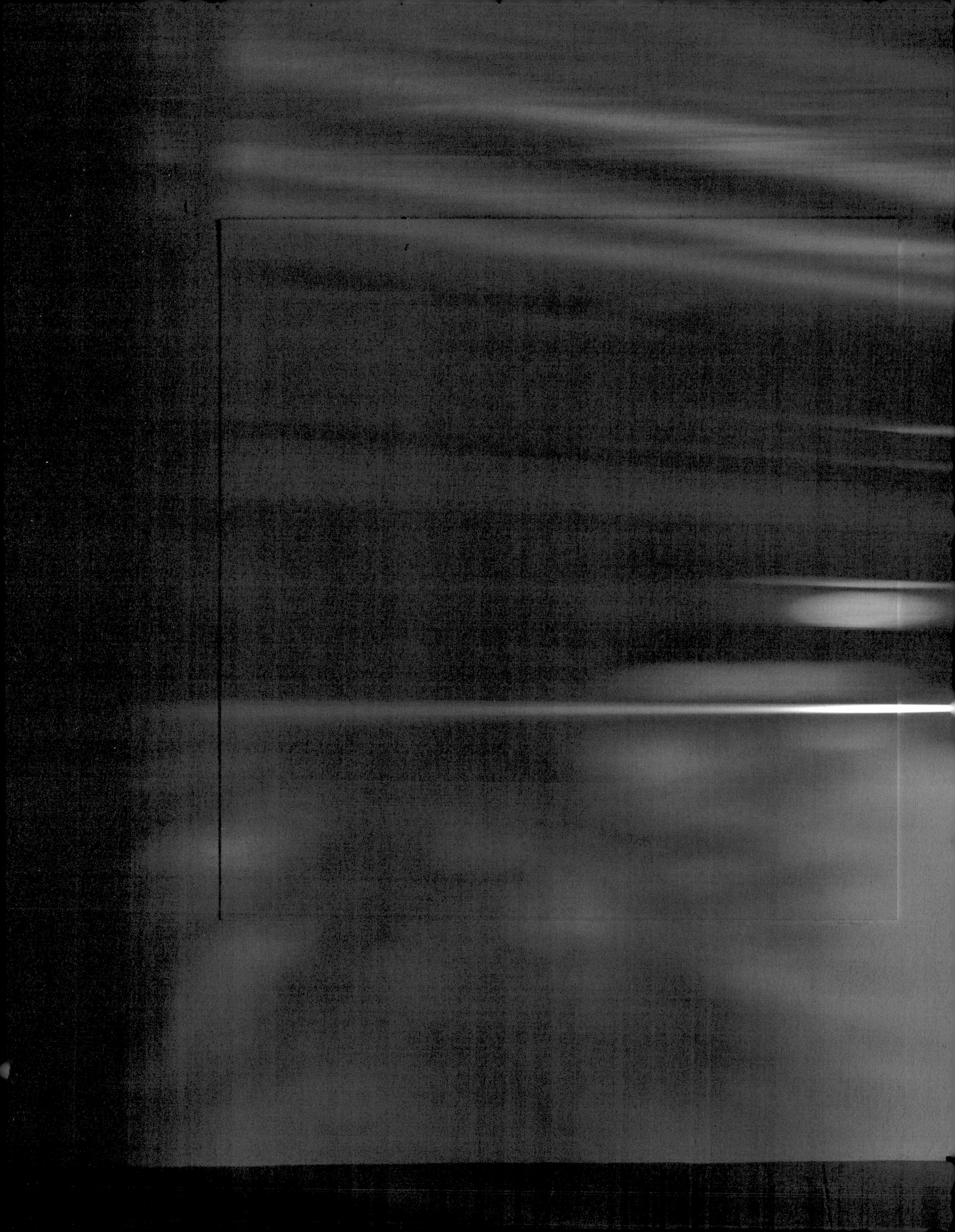

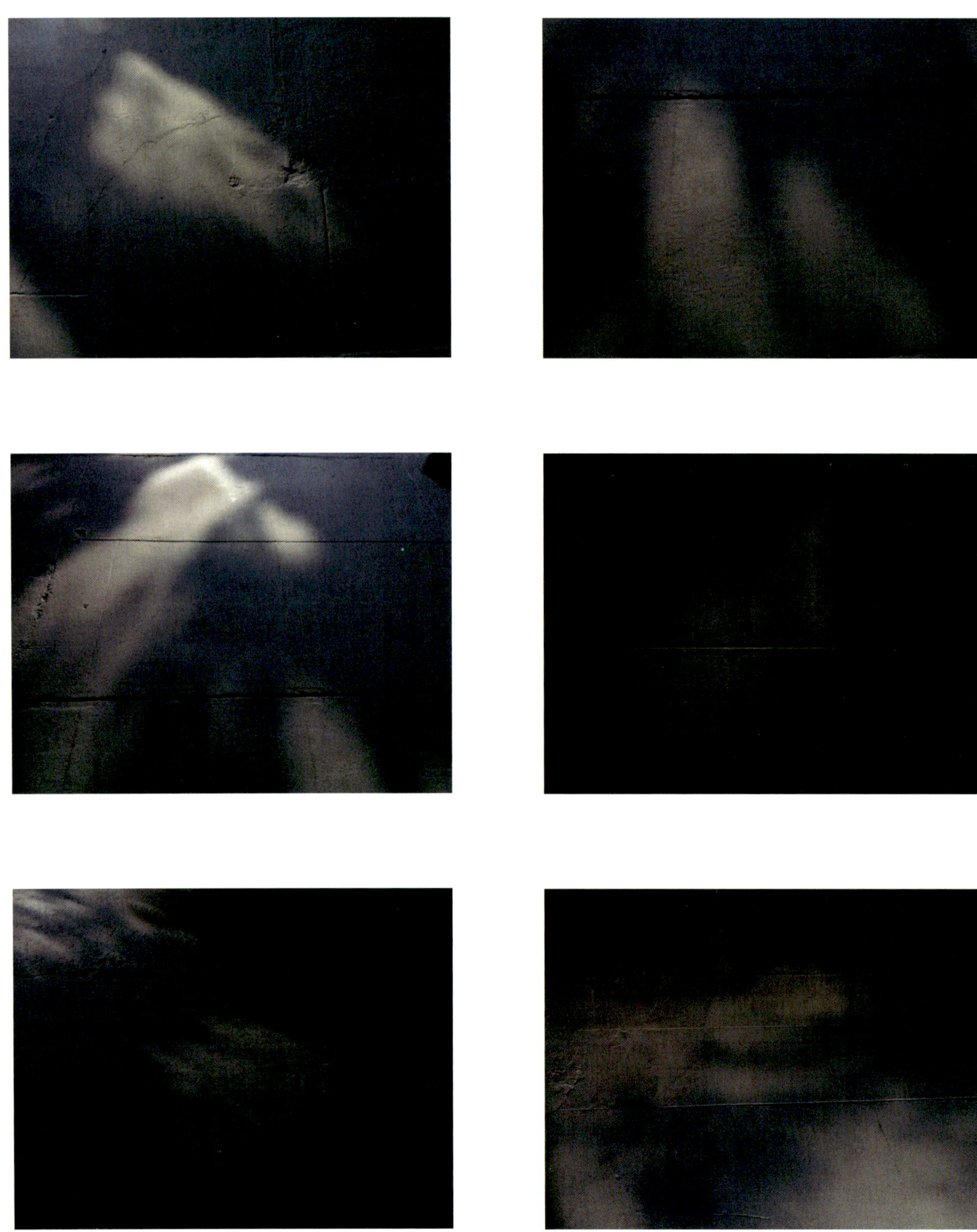

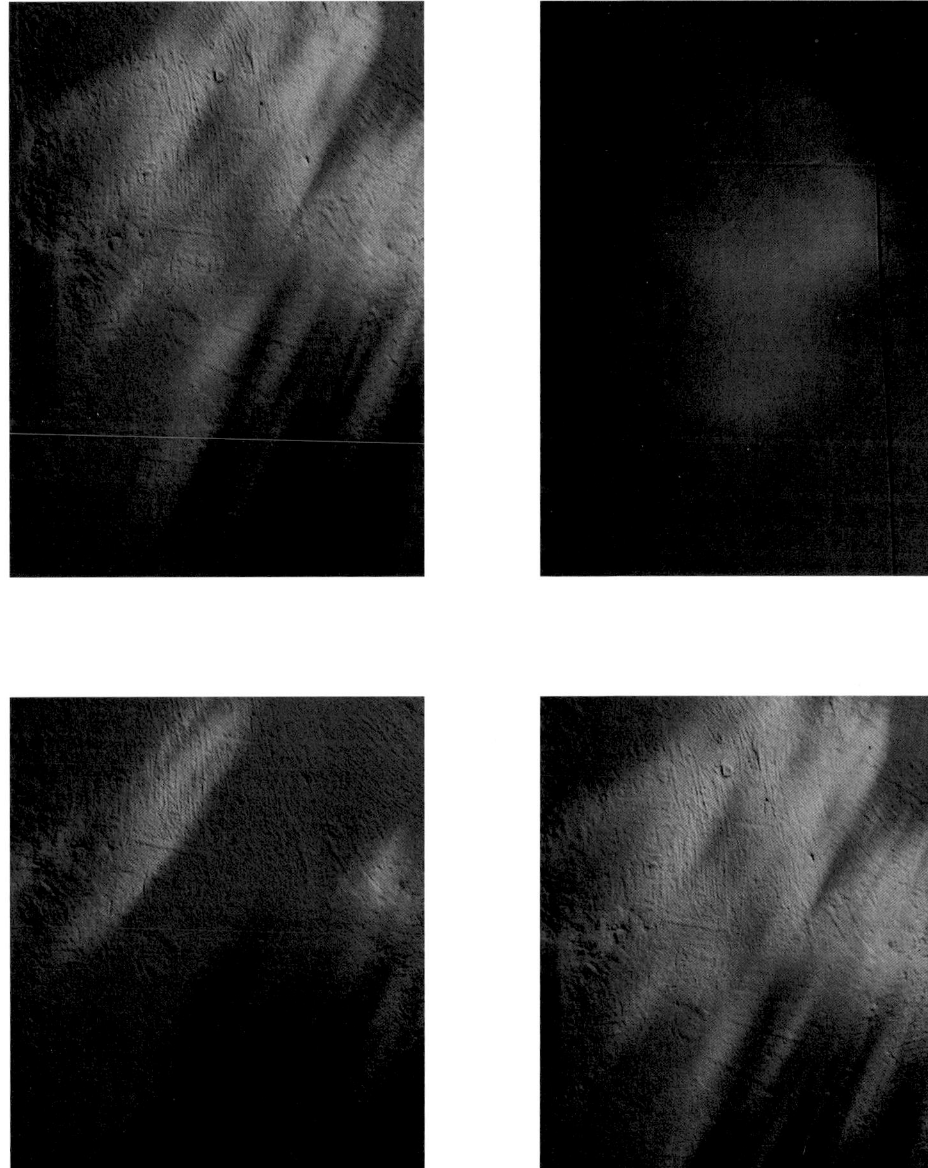

 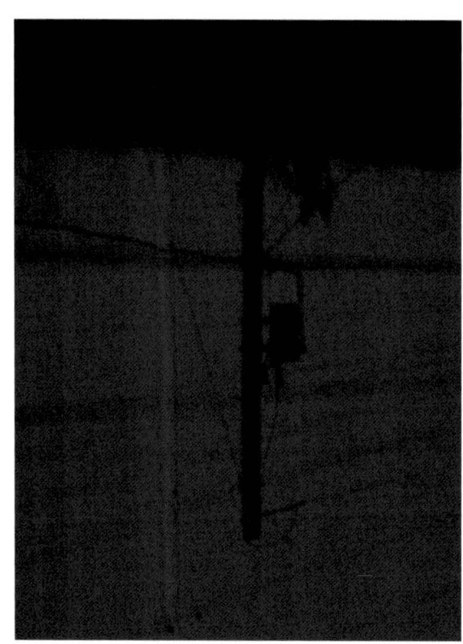

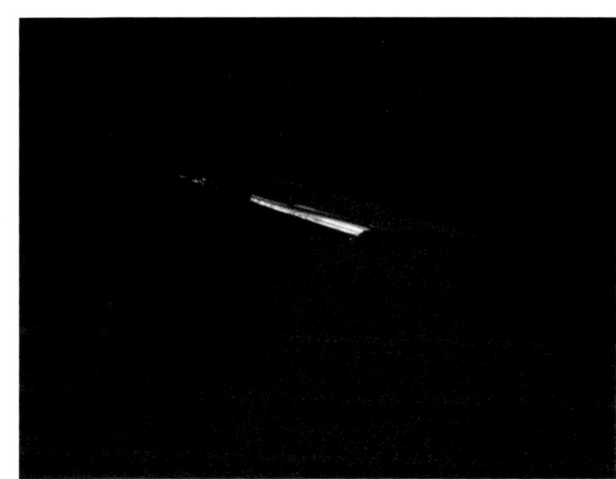
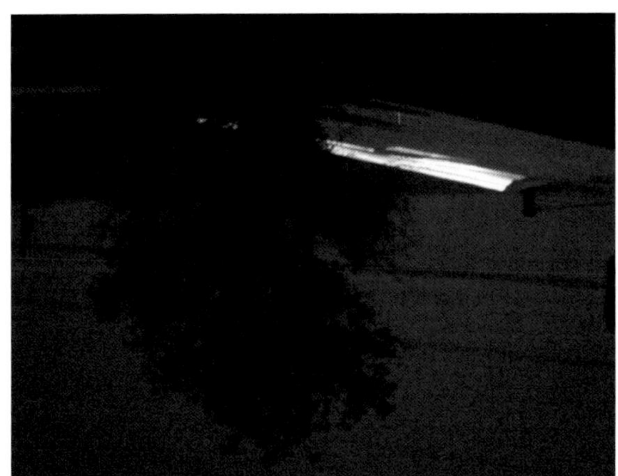
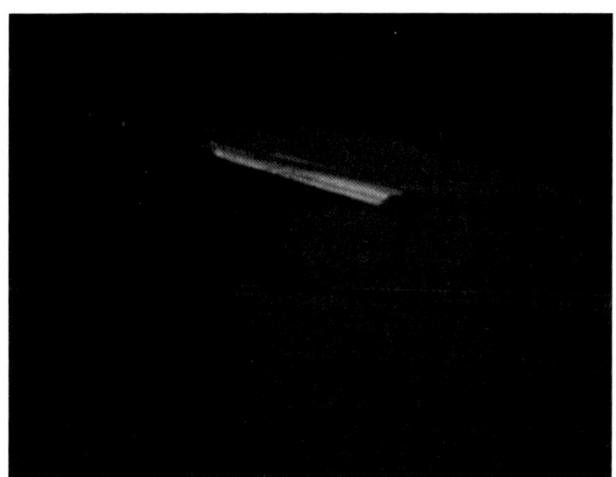

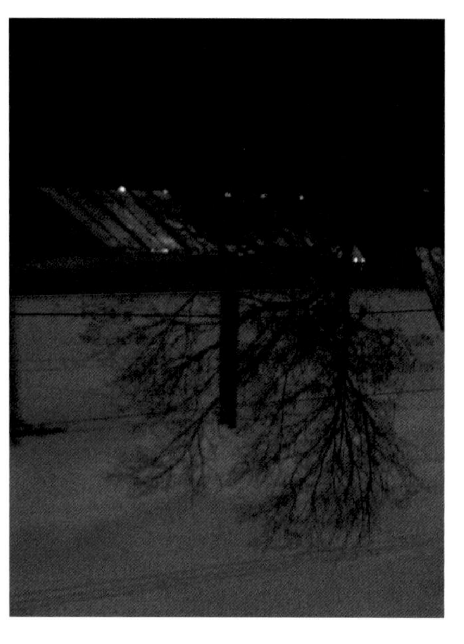

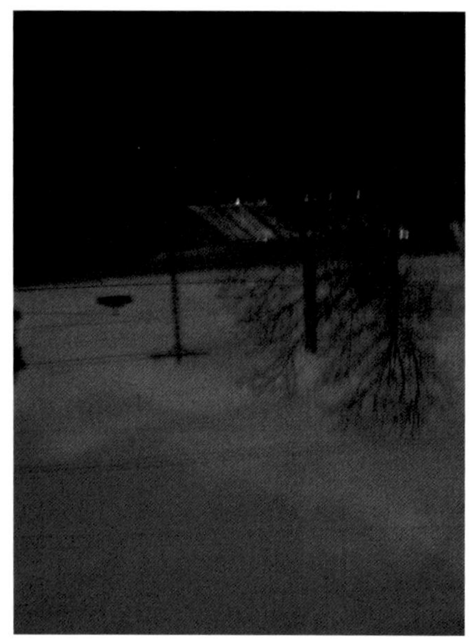
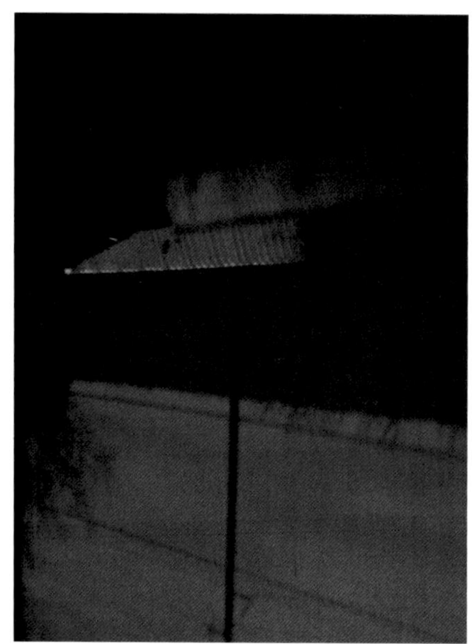

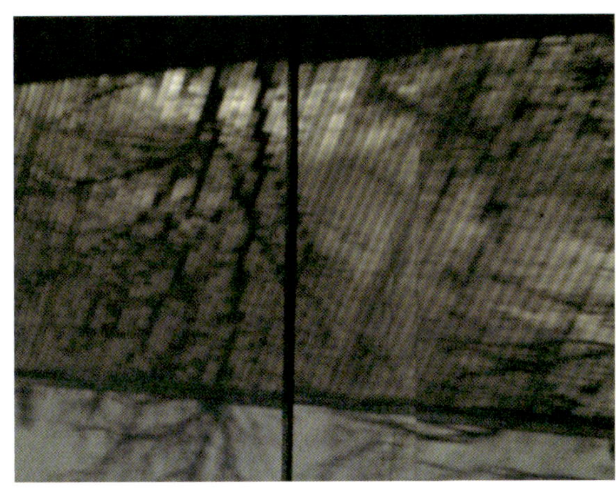

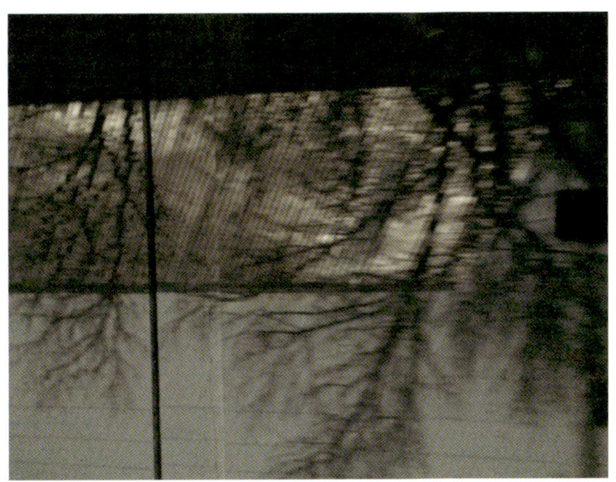

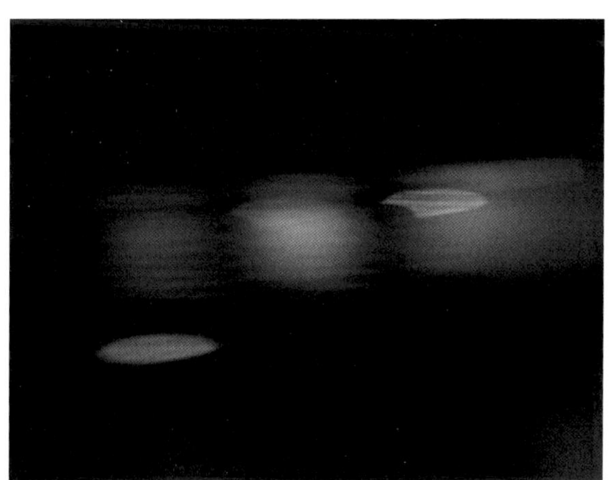

Lost Horizon

Suzanne Hudson

In 2004, I knew of Marfa, but had never visited. So, for me, it represented a latter-day version of the Tibetan lamasery that James Hilton immortalized as Shangri-La in his novel *Lost Horizon* (1933): a place of allegorical more than actual possibility. Yet it is very much a real place. The seat of Presidio County in West Texas, Marfa is rumored to have borrowed its name from a character in Fyodor Dostoyevsky's *The Brothers Karamazov* (the wife of a railroad executive was reading the book and supposedly suggested it, together with names for nearby towns along the Southern Pacific construction route). Beyond boasting a fabled Hollywood pedigree—George Stevens, for example, there filmed *Giant*, an Academy award–winning film starring Elizabeth Taylor, James Dean, and Rock Hudson; more recently, the Coen brothers put the scenery to use in their adaptation of Cormac McCarthy's *No Country for Old Men*—the town is known for its mysterious Marfa Lights, which have been variously attributed to UFOs, Apache spirits, and swamp gas. Marfa's proximity to Big Bend National Park has long been a boon. It became a place of pilgrimage of yet another sort after Donald Judd settled there in 1972.

In 1979, with the help of Dia Art Foundation, Judd purchased a 340-acre parcel that included the abandoned buildings of the former U.S. Army fort D. A. Russell— a remnant of the region's military entanglements, from the Mexican Revolution through World War II. Judd appropriated the cavernous spaces of these facilities for the production and display of his own artworks, in addition to those of peers: initially, Dan Flavin and John Chamberlain and, subsequently, others, including Carl Andre, Roni Horn, Ilya Kabakov, Richard Long, Claes Oldenburg and Coosje van Bruggen, and John Wesley. Judd envisioned a place that could maintain the specificity of the works on view in relation to the surrounding landscape, far from all else. Which is all to say that the very fact of the town's remoteness contributed to its folklore.

John Waters made this point somewhat differently in *Visit Marfa* (2003), a game send-up in which he assumes the region's cultishness to be a consequence of its inaccessibility. I first became aware of the potential of Marfa's becoming a cliché when Waters's broadsheet was reproduced as cover art for *Artforum*'s summer 2004 issue. It trumpets attractions ("See Donald Judd's Bed!"; "Eat Food All the Same Color!") in wink-wink junky typography. Despite the exuberant letter balloons and bold, primary palette, much less the all-American nuclear family pictured on holiday, the tone is dark; trading on the misbegotten spirituality then dominating the reception of certain strains of 1960s practice, Waters dubs Marfa the "Jonestown of Minimalism," also noting as further solicitation the possibility to "scare the locals." Gallows humor, this, for a touristic enterprise predicated on spinning the most astringent of nonobjective modes into vacation amusement, *Visit Marfa* additionally advertises the contents of the magazine it fronts. (This issue of *Artforum* features reviews of Judd's posthumous retrospective at the Tate Modern, among others.) Marfa's star turn thus marked a near apotheosis of Minimalism and coincided with the 2003 opening of Dia:Beacon, which houses Dia Art Foundation's collection of art—including, notably, that of Judd—from the 1960s to the present.

On this occasion, Dia's cofounder Heiner Friedrich declared that "art has no history" and that "there is only a continuous present,"[1] thereby echoing in structure if not content Michael Fried's now-famous invective against Minimalism, penned in 1967. Less retrospective than anticipatory—even prescriptive in his advocating for modernist autonomy past its expiration date—Fried argues for the need for art to make itself available all at once, thereby constituting a "continuous and perpetual present."[2] "Presentness," as Fried so memorably concludes, "is grace."[3] While writers have spilled a great deal of ink on "Art and Objecthood," it is generally acknowledged that Fried understood something fundamental about Minimalism to attack it so cunningly. This means that subsequent positions have often reversed the values associated with his critique—in short, Minimalism is good for the reasons Fried says it is bad—without reconceiving the grounds from which he claimed it. This art was theatrical, by which Fried intended that it was too unbounded, too seeking of address (i.e., even a seemingly independent cube awaits human interaction to activate it). For Fried, it was too situational and too contingent; just so for Friedrich—but for the better.

* * *

Perhaps what I have written to this point seems oblique to the work that I address in what follows. But I am beginning thus because I have come to feel that the setting of Marfa is integral to Zoe Leonard's *100 North Nevill Street* (2013), the fifth camera obscura the artist has fashioned since 2011, when she commenced the series by fitting a lens into the window of Galerie Gisela Capitain in Cologne.

Each of Leonard's cameras has played very specifically with the determinants of architecture, environmental conditions, and place—place, I should clarify, comprising the residue of histories accumulated as images moving across a gallery's skin. Locations for which Leonard has made an oculus also include New York's Highline-crossed Chelsea, rising above the once-cruised West Side piers, and Venice's splendorous Grand Canal, whose waters roil with docking vaporetti. In Marfa, Leonard adapted the cavernous space of an abandoned ice plant that is now part of Chinati Foundation, a contemporary art institution conceived and founded by Judd. Like the vast horizontal spaces of the American West bisected by a still-operational railroad track, which Leonard isolates here, the other camera sites conjoin the mercantile and the touristic only to subsume them both under the sign of art: Chelsea as art district; Venice as art motif; Marfa as art town.

Reminiscent of *You see I am here after all* (2008), a site-specific installation at Dia:Beacon, for which Leonard assembled found postcards of Niagara Falls and configured them into an extensive sequence of grids arranged according to standard views of the natural wonder, *100 North Nevill Street* is remarkably reflexive about its situation. If the former project trades on the legacies of the Hudson River School, indigenous to the Beacon environs, the latter—with its apposition to the arid expanses of the Texan landscape that Judd had so compellingly framed—asserts the continuing relevance of Minimalism. In a statement highlighted on the Chinati Foundation's website, Judd wrote:

> It takes a great deal of time and thought to install work carefully. This should
> not always be thrown away. Most art is fragile and some should be placed and

never moved again. Somewhere a portion of contemporary art has to exist as an example of what the art and its context were meant to be. Somewhere, just as the platinum-iridium meter guarantees the tape measure, a strict measure must exist for the art of this time and place.[4]

100 North Nevill Street is exemplary of Judd's mandate, though it also exceeds it. Life refuses to stay still, and context in Judd's sense is a moving target, however fixed the apparatus for apprehending it.

Leonard takes a lens and a darkened room and makes of them a world contiguous with that directly outside, since on the most basic level the external view produces the possibility for observation within. Walking into the vestibule Leonard constructed, out of the bright, dry high-desert light, effects disorientation. Transition to the cool darkness is protracted, though gradually there comes the awareness that one is enveloped in image—an image of upturned topography, at that—where it seemed there was nothing. Once habituated, figures reveal themselves from grounds, as meaningful incidents in the abiding formlessness that the occurrences punctuate. Movement comes readily in the shapes of clouds moving across the forever sky, occasional pedestrian passersby, and trains passing—their Judd box-like cars suspended upside down as they glide across the long, dominant wall and those adjacent to it; it shows the camera to be alive to incident, even as the lens remains static, transmitting the present continuously.

Despite their communication of instantaneousness, Leonard's cameras have the canny effect of being asynchronous with what they project. Structural changes happen too slowly for us to notice them. They often appear or return to us as representation, when the hour is late. That was also part of the point of Leonard's great *Analogue* (1998–2009), for which, over the span of eleven years, she documented Manhattan's Lower East Side with an old Rolleiflex camera, assembling an archive of some four hundred images revealing the disappearance of markets and individually owned businesses, as well as the larger and more geographically dispersed trade routes that subsumed these singular storefronts and oddly specific goods. Less didactic than elegiac, *Analogue* pays tribute to the technology it names.

100 North Nevill Street accumulates so many comparably transitory moments without fixing or framing them. Representation, save for amalgamations of effects garnered over time, is thus impossible. The camera obscura is prephotographic, a return to source—the dark chamber is both an analogy for the human mind and the unconscious and a functional aspect of the mechanics of sight, wherein light lands on the retina, to be inverted and reversed by the brain—that obviates distinctions between analog and digital photography. Thus it raises questions of photography's object precisely by eschewing its instantiation as a photograph, a material thing. Leonard presents it not as a picture but as a tool. Or better, the camera obscura as Leonard practices it is less a technology than a description of how that world has and continues to generate conventions of picturing. So it becomes a method.

Camera obscuras have traditionally been constructed to focus images onto bounded supports; Leonard, by contrast, allows the light to spill through her lens into the whole environment—walls, I beams, and floors alike. The features of the architecture become decisive to the emergence of form, which it interrupts. A perfect picture is impossible, for, along with a ladder and other concessions to 100 North Nevill's former use, even pragmatic elements as small and seemingly inconsequential as rivets dotting a vertical post skew planarity. This intercession is not only a matter of aesthetics, even if textures and colors are at stake. No passive screen, the warehouse everywhere is a self-determining material context. And this context coincides with the visible "content" of a landscape of use scarred by machines and worked by ranchers that the camera brings inside, which is a kind of context, too, as Judd insisted. As noted above, 100 North Nevill was long the site of the production of ice for use in shipping goods out of Marfa. It still sits at the outskirts of town, near the highway. Freight trains run east and west along the track, ferrying oil, gas, and cattle. One never knows from which direction or at what time a train might pass, heightening the sense of anticipation felt with each sonorous whistle.

A kind of medium in its own right, the building carries sounds, such as these signals, which it conducts through its metal scaffolding. Imperfectly fitted into their casements, shabby windows lend the building a porosity that confuses interior and exterior: the hum of a power station and the intermittent songs of birds, skids of tires, or squeals of children are distinct, and so make their sources seem significantly closer than they in fact are. The sounds imply action, which is not always visible, much of it occurring, as it were, just off-screen (e.g., though it isn't proximate enough to the lens to be registered visually, a playground down the block provides a sound track). As the light that streams through the lens diminishes and the darkness renders sight impossible, sounds become differently important. Fundamentally representational, the camera has profound lapses, and not just after dusk—moments of abstraction, where color somehow fails to organize into an image or light remains too diffuse to register detail. Even when the projection is crisp in parts of the image, it is not uniformly so, as it blurs or is thrown into shadow elsewhere. This is to say nothing of the intervention of bodies in the image, a frequent event since Leonard conspicuously puts the lens at eye level to make the mechanism transparent.

Contingency is perhaps inherent to art, and exigencies of looking at it are the norm. (The art historian T. J. Clark performs this inconstancy in his book-length meditation on visiting two paintings by Poussin daily and trying to put his mercurial experiences of them into words.)[5] Nonetheless, Leonard's use of the camera radicalizes this tendency. For every aspect or vantage, there is another, and none is privileged; for every glimpse, there could be, and one feels acutely that there will be, so many others missed. The atmosphere shifts. The days pass, and the seasons change. Conditions are specific and likely unrepeatable. Each moment seems portentous. This is Fried's bad dream of Minimalism, infinite duration wherein there is only irresolution. Radically dependent on outside forces, the camera's projections imply no telos, nor do they offer the comforts of finitude. With each blink, the world is still there, albeit in a configuration different—however minutely—from how it was before.

Because of this, Leonard's camera conjures yet another model of photography, namely the sequential photographs of Eadweard Muybridge, which capture the movements of a horse galloping; men engaged in farm, construction, or domestic work; martial maneuvers; and sport. Despite his patent attention to it, action for

Muybridge might be said to exist apart from a narrative other than that of the process by which it was generated. However dramatic the scenario, there is neither climax nor denouement. Dan Graham compellingly described this horizontality, an equivalence of moments causally related, writing of Muybridge's shots: "Every thing is in the present—present entirely on the surface. No moment is created; things—moments—are sufficient unto themselves. Things are separated from other things and no thing is more important than any other thing."[6] (Of course, the images themselves are now historical, beholden to a robust historiography that involves their being written into stories of other kinds.)

One of the conceits of James Hilton's book *Lost Horizon* is that the inhabitants of his city experience longevity, though they are not protected once they leave the lamasery's walls. Writing on the cusp of World War II, Hilton must have seen Shangri-La as a fortress capable of withstanding incursions from without: a safe haven for culture. Only a few years later, in 1939, Clement Greenberg published his watershed "Avant-Garde and Kitsch," a tract holding forth a remarkably similar argument for the maintenance of high culture in the face of war. Such shoring up is perhaps symptomatic of its decade. Yet it bears mention that Greenberg would later write "The Recentness of Sculpture." Published the same year as Fried's "Art and Objecthood," Greenberg's later essay revisited many of the same themes that his earlier text addressed. (Indeed, James Meyer has written of the later text as an explicit updating of "Avant-Garde and Kitsch.")[7] In many ways, Judd's objectives do not contradict this. To the contrary, his notion of permanence—a strict measure, in his words, against which works disposed elsewhere could be assessed—presumes the necessity of maintenance, even care, in the face of, if not punctual cataclysm, then the more benign if no less entropic passage of time. *100 North Nevill Street* proposes instead the satiety of moments, one thing after the next. A sentinel watching things go by, it is indifferent to us, even as it exists for our witnessing. The whole world hangs there, as if in wait, until one day it doesn't.

NOTES

1. Heiner Friedrich, quoted in Hal Foster, "At Dia:Beacon," *London Review of Books* 25, no. 11 (June 5, 2003): 29.

2. Michael Fried, "Art and Objecthood" (1967), in *Art and Objecthood: Essays and Reviews* (Chicago: University of Chicago Press, 1998), 172.

3. Ibid.

4. Donald Judd, quoted in "Chinati: Mission and History," http://www.chinati.org/visit/missionhistory.php, accessed December 20, 2013.

5. T. J. Clark, *The Sight of Death: An Experiment in Art Writing* (New Haven: Yale University Press, 2006).

6. Dan Graham, "Muybridge Moments: From Here to There?," *Arts* 41, no. 4 (February 1967): 24.

7. James Meyer, *Minimalism: Art and Polemics in the 1960s* (New Haven: Yale University Press, 2004), 211.

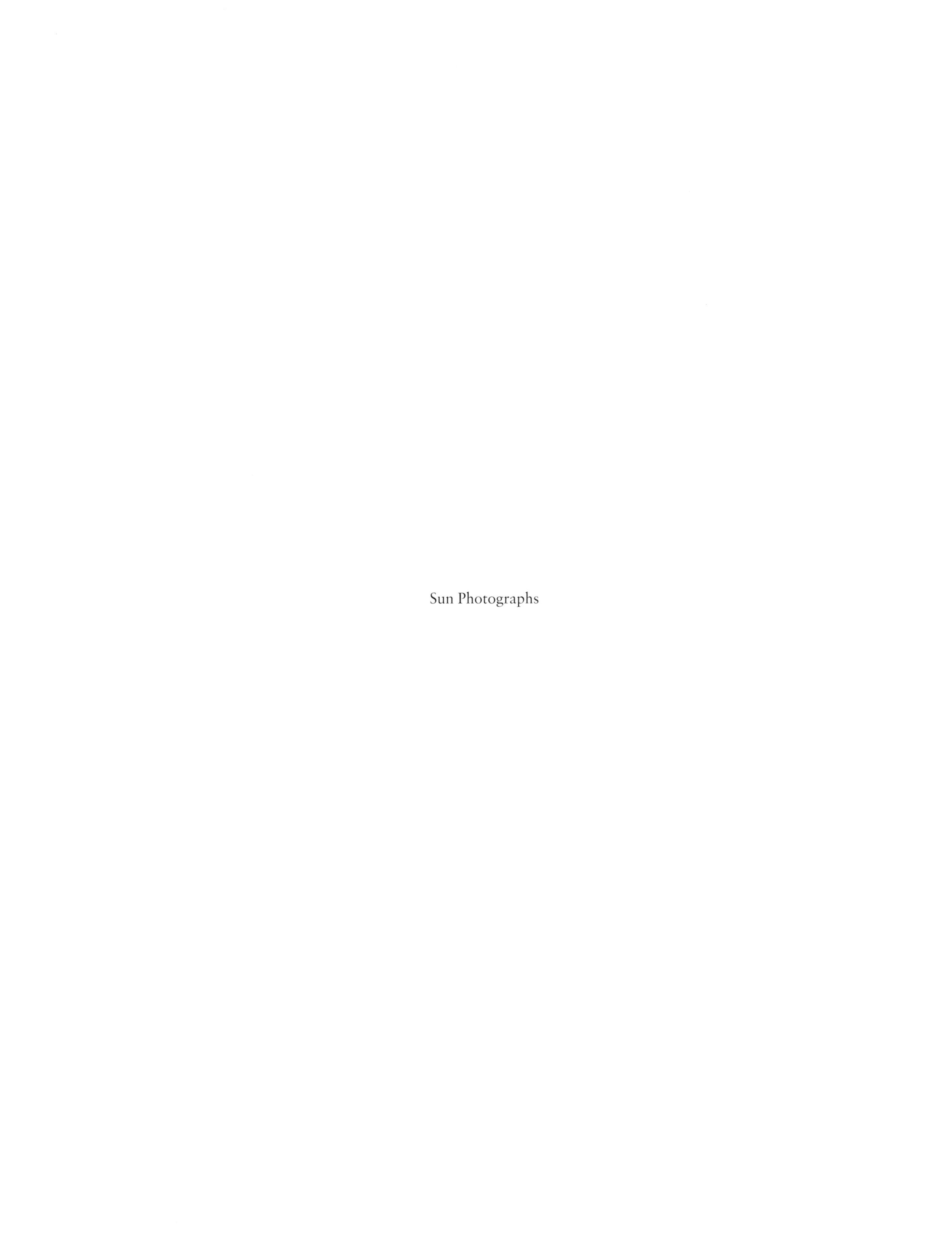

Sun Photographs

Where the Feeling and Everything Is

Glenn Ligon

In *Straight, No Chaser*, a documentary about the life and career of jazz pianist Thelonious Monk, tenor saxophonist and longtime collaborator Charlie Rouse comments on Monk's habit of including only certain takes of a recording session on a resulting album. "We start out and we do a take," Rouse said, "and usually we take the first take, sometimes the second, but never the third. [Monk] said once you play it the first time, that's where the feeling and everything is and after that it starts going downhill." And if you mess up? "That's your problem," Rouse continued. "You have to hear that all the rest of your life." While said with a jocularity typical of Monk's collaborators (and Monk himself), Rouse's comments reveal that for Monk the album is a vehicle for the transmission of feelings. A record is an object through which musicians and audience meet and the conveyance of feelings—privileged over technical perfection and individual virtuosity—is its highest purpose. In this light, the much-discussed idiosyncrasies and difficulty of Monk's music can be seen as pushing the music toward where "the feeling and everything is," which reflects not only the way Monk assessed the merits of particular takes but also a musical ethos that he took seriously over the course of his entire career.

In a 2008 discussion with curator Lynne Cooke, Zoe Leonard talked about the relationship between a photographer, an image, and a viewer. The camera, Leonard claims, is a stand-in for the photographer's body, for her perspective on the world. As a result, a viewer's encounter with an image is also an encounter with the photographer. "I'm always there because I saw it, and you are always there because you are looking at it," Leonard explains. "The image is the fulcrum point where your view and my view meet." The image, as the fulcrum, functions in a similar way as a record does for Monk: as a site of connection between artist and audience. Like Monk, Leonard favors the encounter over conventional notions of "good" photography. Leonard has said that she wants to "draw the viewer into the process of looking, so we can look at these things together." This is not only to show you what she sees but also to draw you into a shared emotion space. To look together is to feel together, even if we don't all feel the same things. But if one were to say that Leonard's images are somehow about "feelings and everything," how would that manifest in the work? For instance, what is it about her photographs of the sun that invites such a reading when there is seemingly so little in the images to connect to? The images somehow *do* have a powerful effect, as I experienced when I first saw them in "Observation Point," Leonard's exhibition at the Camden Arts Centre in London in spring 2012. Pinned directly to the walls of a long room illuminated by enormous skylights, the photographs triggered a kind of melancholy in me, one so strong that as I surveyed the work I began to sing "Everyday is like Sunday / Everyday is silent and gray," the chorus to a Morrissey song about the end of the world. Usually photos of the sun provoke emotions that are the opposite of melancholy, as countless numbers of sunrise and sunset images posted on social-media sites and used in advertising demonstrate. While we might assume that the sun photographs were taken during the harsh light of day (Leonard wore a welding mask while shooting to protect her eyes), the images nevertheless have a vexed relationship to both amateur and commercial photography, as they invite identification and emotional connection while refusing the conventions of composition, color, printing, and display those genres employ. It is by this refusal that Leonard's sun photographs transform something we presume we already know—the sun—and make it strange.

* * *

Leonard has said that an image is the fulcrum at which photographer and viewer meet, but in the case of the sun photographs, what, exactly, is depicted in these images where we meet? The subject of the series provides a clue, but the diversity of images that fall under it makes it difficult to judge with any precision. For example, *December 3, frame 3* (2011/2012) shows a relatively distinct, medium-size orb of light slightly below the midpoint of the photograph. Above it on the right is a much smaller point of light, which in turn has a fainter, haloed orb sitting just above it. While some of these spots are the result of lens flare, in the context of such spare images each detail commands our attention and throws into question our certainty about the focal point of the image. In *January 23, frame 8* (2011) the sun is depicted as a small, ethereal disc floating in a gray sea of mist. Indeed, the light is so diffuse one could easily mistake the image for that of the moon. Although each photograph is unmistakably part of the series, the sometimes radical differences between them make it hard to believe they all have the same subject matter, except for the one overarching motif, which is light. They seem to be susceptible to the Rashomon effect; it is as if Leonard asked different people to look briefly at the sun and then describe what they saw, and the resulting images are an artist's rendering of those eyewitness accounts.

* * *

While on the surface the images are spare, giving us no landscape, figure, or evocative title to anchor ourselves in, the sparseness is used as a means to focus our attention. This applies to not only what the photographs depict but how they are exhibited. "The material aspect of the photograph," Leonard has said, "also communicates some of what it is," and the display of the sun photographs makes clear that we are meant to consider them as objects, not only images. Unglazed and pinned directly to the wall at the Camden Arts Centre, the photographs assumed a quality of vulnerability that they would not have had if they had been matted and framed. The presentation was, in part, a solution to a practical problem—glass would have caused distracting reflections. But the hanging also highlighted the ways the photos were subject to conditions in the exhibition space, where dust, humidity, and a viewer's touch could all have had an effect. Breaking from museum exhibition protocols, the installation engendered a closer scrutiny and a more nuanced reading of the photographs, one made more vivid by the nakedness of their display. Another aspect of the installation that broke from the norm was the amount of light in the gallery. Usually photographs are shown under subdued light to prevent fading. Leonard chose an opposite strategy: letting light flood in through the seven enormous skylights and scheduling the show to occur when there would be the most daylight. The effect of this was to merge the subject of the photographs with the mode of their display, creating the sense of being immersed in both light and its photographic representation.

* * *

Besides light, the sun photographs have another subject matter: time. To take a photograph is to start a process. For Leonard, that means shooting several rolls of film, making enlarged contact sheets, creating work prints of promising images, selecting a few to develop further, then making more specific, finely tuned prints of a particular image until the size, paper, tone, density, grain visibility, and contrast, among other details, are finalized. The dust and occasional scratches on the negative that appear on the final print all speak to her working with an image over time and accepting the inevitable marks of that process. Even the titles, which record the date the photo was taken and its frame number, serve as indicators of time, locating the images within the process of their own making. Leonard has said that her art "works with time and accepts time as a medium," and the sun photographs are another iteration of her concern with the temporal. Yet Leonard doesn't let this concern veer into nostalgia. Because of her attention to the viewing conditions and choices about framing and display, the experience of the photographs is an encounter with objects in real time. To be sure, like any photograph, they are a record of the past, but the feelings they invoke remain stubbornly in the present.

* * *

Palinopsia (from the Greek *palin* ["again"] and *opsia* ["seeing"]) is a condition that causes afterimages in the eye to remain long after the stimulus that caused them has disappeared. For a long time after I first saw the sun photographs, an afterimage of the sun was burned onto my retina. It was an image not of the sun I could see traversing the sky on any given day but of the one I saw in Leonard's photographs. Silvery gray, fugitive, diffuse, this afterimage persisted long after I had seen the show, and gradually I got used to this second sight, one that complemented the ways in which I normally look. The sun photographs were a kind of double vision: when I saw the sun in the sky I saw the sun in Leonard's photos, and the two were different and the same. The light of the sun itself became the fulcrum where we met.

January 27, frame 8, 2012
Gelatin silver print
36 ½ x 29 ½ inches

February 27, frame 11, 2012
Gelatin silver print
13⅜ x 19 inches

February 27, frame 30, 2012
Gelatin silver print
14 x 9⅞ inches

January 23, frame 8, 2011
Gelatin silver print
22 x 31¼ inches

April 5, frame 10, 2011
Gelatin silver print
16 ¼ x 22 ⅞ inches

December 3, frame 3, 2011/2012
Gelatin silver print
30½ x 24¾ inches

April 4, frame 2, 2011
Gelatin silver print
21 ⅜ x 30 ¼ inches

August 6, frame 19, 2011/2012
Gelatin silver print
27⅜ x 19⅜ inches

August 4, frame 9, 2011/2012
Gelatin silver print
23¾ x 17¼ inches

Images

Cover:
February 27, frame 25, 2012
Gelatin silver print
13⅞ x 9¾ inches

Frontispiece:
iPhone photograph by Zoe Leonard

Pages 19–29:
St. Apern Straße 26, 2011
Galerie Gisela Capitain, Cologne
September 9–October 29, 2011
Photographs by Lothar Schnepf

Pages 32–49:
Arkwright Road, 2012
Camden Arts Centre, London
March 31–June 24, 2012
Pages 32–43: photographs by Richard Shellabear, Todd-White Art Photography
Pages 44–49: iPhone photographs by Zoe Leonard

Pages 52–61:
Campo San Samuele, 3231, 2012
François Pinault Foundation, Palazzo Grassi, Venice
August 30, 2012–January 13, 2013
Pages 52–55: photographs by Lothar Schnepf
Pages 56–61: iPhone photographs by Zoe Leonard

Pages 64–81:
453 West 17th Street, 2012
Murray Guy, New York
September 15–October 27, 2012
Pages 64–71: photographs by Bill Jacobson
Pages 72–81: photographs by Zoe Leonard and Sadie Benning

Pages 90–121:
100 North Nevill Street, 2013
Chinati Foundation, Marfa, Texas
December 15, 2013–December 2014
Pages 90–111: photographs by Fredrik Nilsen
Pages 112–21: iPhone photographs by Zoe Leonard

Pages 130–35:
Installation views, "Observation Point," Camden Arts Centre, London, March 31–June 24, 2012
Photographs by Richard Shellabear, Todd-White Art Photography

Pages 141–57:
Sun photographs
Courtesy the artist; Galerie Gisela Capitain, Cologne; Murray Guy, New York; and Galleria
Raffaella Cortese, Milan

Contributors

Diedrich Diederichsen is an author, music journalist, and cultural critic who lives and works in Berlin and Vienna. His wide-ranging writings, which address subjects as diverse as contemporary art, modern composition, cinema, theater, design, and politics, have been published in a variety of books, magazines, and journals, including *Texte zur Kunst*, *Der Tagesspiegel*, *Artscribe*, *Artforum*, and *Frieze*. His most recent books include *The Whole Earth: California and the Disappearance of the Outside* (Berlin: Sternberg Press, 2013), edited with Anselm Franke, and *Utopia of Sound* (Vienna: Schleebrügge, 2010), edited with Constanze Ruhm. Diederichsen is professor of theory, practice, and communication at the Academy of Fine Art, Vienna.

Suzanne Hudson currently teaches contemporary art at the University of Southern California, Los Angeles. She is a cofounder of the Contemporary Art Think Tank and the Society of Contemporary Art Historians, an affiliate society of the College Art Association, for which she currently serves as president emerita and chair of the Executive Committee. Hudson's work has appeared in such publications as *Parkett*, *Flash Art*, *Art Journal*, and *October*; a regular contributor to *Artforum* since 2004, she also has written numerous essays for international exhibition catalogues and artist monographs and lectured widely. She is the author of *Robert Ryman: Used Paint* (MIT Press, 2009; 2011) and a coeditor of *Contemporary Art: 1989–Present* (Wiley-Blackwell, 2013). Her book *Painting Now* is forthcoming from Thames & Hudson.

Zoe Leonard lives and works in New York. An artist who works primarily with photography and sculpture, she has exhibited extensively since the late 1980s. Selected solo exhibitions include *100 North Nevill Street*, Chinati Foundation, Marfa, Texas (2013–14); "Observation Point," Camden Arts Centre, London (2012); "Photographs," Fotomuseum Winterthur (2007), which traveled to Museo Nacional Centro de Arte Reina Sofía in Madrid (2008), Museum moderner Kunst Stifting Ludwig Wien in Vienna (2009), and Pinakothek der Moderne in Munich (2009); *You see I am here after all,* Dia:Beacon, Beacon, New York (2008); "Derrotero," Dia at the Hispanic Society, New York (2008); *Analogue,* the Wexner Center for the Arts, Columbus, Ohio, and Villa Arson, Nice (2007); Centre National de la Photographie, Paris (1998); *Strange Fruit*, Philadelphia Museum of Art (1998); Kunsthalle Basel (1997); Secession, Vienna (1997); and the Renaissance Society at the University of Chicago (1993). Leonard's works have been included in numerous group exhibitions, including Documenta 9 (1992), Documenta 12 (2007), and the 1993, 1997, and 2014 Whitney Biennials. Leonard's writing has appeared in *October, Texte zur Kunst*, and *LTTR* and in books on Agnes Martin, James Castle, and Josiah McElheny. She is a founding member of the feminist artist collective fierce pussy and is cochair of photography at the Milton Avery Graduate School of the Arts at Bard College.

Glenn Ligon is an artist who lives and works in New York. A midcareer retrospective of Ligon's work, "Glenn Ligon: America," opened at the Whitney Museum of American Art in 2011 and traveled to the Los Angeles County Museum of Art and the Modern Art Museum of Fort Worth. Ligon has been the subject of solo museum exhibitions at the Power Plant, Toronto; the Walker Art Center, Minneapolis; the Studio Museum in Harlem, New York; the Institute of Contemporary Art, University of Pennsylvania, Philadelphia; and the Kunstverein Munich. His work was included in Documenta 11 (2002) and the 1991 and 1993 Whitney Biennials. Ligon has earned numerous awards, including the Joan Mitchell Foundation Grant, the John Simon Guggenheim Memorial Foundation Fellowship, the Skowhegan Medal for Painting, and the Studio Museum's Joyce Alexander Wein Artist Prize.

Eileen Myles is a poet, novelist, and art journalist who lives in New York. She's the author of more than twenty volumes of poetry, fiction, plays, performances, libretti, and essays, and her collected art writing, *The Importance of Being Iceland: Travel Essays in Art* (Semiotext(e), 2009), which was supported by a Creative Capital/Warhol Foundation grant, is already regarded as a classic of its kind. Myles is a Guggenheim fellow and a 2014 recipient of a grant from the Foundation for Contemporary Arts.

Zoe Leonard: Available Light

The artist thanks: Diedrich Diederichsen, Suzanne Hudson, Eileen Myles, Glenn Ligon, Karen Kelly, Barbara Schröder, Joseph Logan, Doro Globus, Bill Jacobson, Freddie Nilsen, Richard Shellabear, Lothar Schnepf, Jenni Lomax, Caroline Bourgeois, Jenny Moore, Rob Weiner, Laurent Girard, Charlie Griffin, Eric Weeks, George T. Keene, Jocelyn Davis, Jonah Groeneboer, Liz Deschenes, Tony Feher, Josiah McElheny, Sadie Benning, Emma Hedditch, Briony Fer, Lynne Cooke, Gregg Bordowitz, Elisabeth Lebovici, Catherine Facerias, and everyone at Galerie Gisela Capitain, Galleria Raffaella Cortese, Murray Guy, Camden Arts Centre, Palazzo Grassi, and the Chinati Foundation.

This book has been made possible with generous funding from Galerie Gisela Capitain, Cologne; Murray Guy, New York; and Galleria Raffaella Cortese, Milan. Additional support has been provided by Nion McEvoy, Karsten Schubert, and Thea Westreich and Ethan Wagner.

Edited by Karen Kelly and Barbara Schröder
Book design by Joseph Logan, New York, assisted by Rachel Hudson
Proofreading by Sam Frank

This book is typeset in Akzidenz-Grotesk and Sabon. The paper is Phoenix Motion Xenon 150 gsm.

Printed and bound by Die Keure, Brugge, Belgium

Published in 2014 by

Dancing Foxes Press
16 Lefferts Place
Brooklyn, New York 11238
United States
www.dfpress.org

Ridinghouse
46 Lexington Street
London W1F 0LP
United Kingdom
www.ridinghouse.co.uk

Distributed in the US by

Distributed in the UK and Europe by

RAM Publications
2525 Michigan Avenue Buliding A2
Santa Monica, CA 90404
United States
www.rampub.com

Cornerhouse
70 Oxford Street
Manchester M1 5NH
United Kingdom
www.cornerhouse.org

First edition 2014
© 2014 Dancing Foxes Press

All artworks © Zoe Leonard
Texts © the authors

British Library Cataloguing-in-Publication Data: a full catalogue record of this book is available from the British Library.

Library of Congress Control Number: 2014930715
ISBN: 978 1 905464 86 9

Printed in Belgium